Middle School Sex Ed....
-or -   "THEY ASKED
YOU WHAT ? !"

by David
Beck
and
Fran
Spokane,
MA-CCC,
Communication
Disorders
Specialist

Adventures in Middle School Sex Education, and Why It's More Important than Ever to Have a Meaningful Sex Talk with Your Kids

Copyright © 2013 David Beck
All rights reserved.
ISBN: 1484034635
ISBN 13: 9781484034637
Library of Congress Control Number: 2013906829
CreateSpace Independent Publishing Platform
North Charleston, South Carolina

DEDICATION

To Frannie: The essential person in my life. The very best friend, wife, muse, lover and source of all wise advice, counsel and encouragement

To Natasha and Nicole: The amazing, lovely daughters that more than anything are testament to Frannie's skill as a mother and shaper of the very best of young, strong women. Watching them grow was a large part of the inspiration for this book

To the wonderful Burke family, the best of friends and cheer-leaders. Special thanks to Nancy Burke and her brother David who gave me wonderful feedback, guidance and direction in pub-lishing this book.

To my fabulous students over the years, who asked all the hilarious, thoughtful and startling questions that made this book possible

And, to my wonderful teaching colleagues and friends who encouraged this book and look forward to each year to when I share some of the choice questions at lunch......

TABLE OF CONTENTS

INTRODUCTION

Some samples from the "TMI" question box (the spelling and punctuation are as received, all clearly written by the same hand):

- *(First slip) What is a cunt?*
- *What is a pussy?*
- *What is a dush?*
- *What is a chod?*
- *(Second slip) What is finguring?*
- *What is an argsim?*
- *What is testicles*
- *What is brestfeeding*
- *(Third slip) What is sperm?*
- *What is a condum?*
- *What is semen?*
- *What is a vigina*
- *What is masterbating*

A couple of related vignettes: During a class work period on our CO_2 Rocket car physics project, kids are in line before my class workdesk as I help them assemble their car kits. A student asks me if they should put WD-40™ on their wheels. I answer, "No, it gums up the plastic tube bearing, use some graphite powder lube instead." Three beats, then a half dozen of the **girls** burst into giggles. The guys still look blank. "Mr. Beck, you said **lube**," the girls laugh when they can get the words out between chuckles. I stare in wonderment, there being no doubt in my mind they know the sexual connotation of the word and find my innocent use of it hilarious. Thirteen and fourteen year old girls know what lube is....

A few weeks later in a different class, as we are setting up for a lab, I tell the kids that a particular equation will be "handy" in working out their calculations. Again, three beats before the two girls seated in front of me crack up.

"He said **handy**!"

"Wait," her friend says, "are you thinking the same way I am?" They put their heads together to exchange quick whispered confirmation, then burst into giggles again. As above, the sexual "hand job" connotation of the term "handy" is obvious in their reaction.

These are not the school "sluts" (don't like that term, but I don't want you to go in that direction). They are sweet, pretty, smart and successful girls. In either case there was no intent to mock or be rude, they just got the un-intended double entendre and couldn't help laughing. Teachers have to mull every word these days.....

The questions, the real world scenarios above, and literally hundreds like them, are what I point to when someone asks me, "Why another sex information book, and **why** one directed at middle school kids?" While adults might have the impression that we're drowning in sexual information, kids are mostly swimming in a sea of incomplete answers and misinformation. The combination of hearsay from their friends, distorted sexual/romantic images from TV and movies, and the impressions they get of sex and sexuality from the Internet leaves them confused and vulnerable. Something else you should know: "sex" and "porn" were the number 4 and 5 most-searched items on the Internet by kids under 18 in 2009. (1)

The examples above show breadth of middle school sexuality, from the lost helplessness of a protected boy's question box slips to the mature awareness of girls who almost certainly technical virgins at least....

Someone had to address this gulf of middle school sexual information and confusion, and it might as well be me, the science and sex ed teacher.

So, I'm going to make some broad, sweeping statements from time to time in this book. Like any broad, sweeping statements, there are exceptions, and I will be the first to say that some of my observations don't apply universally to all children in every part of the United States. But I'm more than willing to bet that they apply to more of your children, nieces, nephews, and neighbors' children than you would be willing to acknowledge, unless you've kept your ears very attuned to the "chatter" (as the intelligence services call the electronic and diplomatic exchanges they monitor) in that exotic, exciting world that teens inhabit.

My central point, however, the BIG THING, the sweeping generality that I want parents and any young teenagers that read this to take away, is this:

However hip you think you are as a parent, your kids are growing up in a sexual environment and culture far removed from the one you may have experienced when you were their age, and eons beyond the "sexual revolution" Baby Boomers brag about pioneering in the 60's and 70's. My very sophisticated daughters, both around 30, are horrified at the clueless sexuality they hear and see in the middle schoolers they encounter. Middle schoolers today, despite often glaring gaps in their knowledge, are hyper-exposed and hyper-aware of our sexual culture, and they experience it as a day-to-day reality, not as something they'll experience in the future or "when they're ready." The fact is, a number of studies and surveys show that between 10% and 15% of 12 to 14 year olds are having sex of some kind. Of course, it's *impossible* that *your* kid would be one of those 10 -15%. However, your kid *is going to school with those kids,* and almost certainly one or more of their truly sweet, delightful friends is one of these sexually active early-mid teens. It's not just the "bad" or "slutty" kids. (2)

You cannot avoid this any longer. Whatever your values, religion, or personal experience with sex, you need to educate your middle schoolers early and often in the responsibilities, realities, and—yes—pleasures of sexuality. If you don't, your kid will be walking into a very adult world of sexual experience armed only with ignorance, what they find on the Internet, and the bravado of teenagers everywhere. You simply cannot take the "not my kid" attitude and hope for the best. In addition, we should all be demanding meaningful, real world sex ed from our school districts. I don't care if you want to teach abstinence. Some will abstain, but pretty much everybody has sex at some point, and if you are going to teach them to abstain, you better give them real facts and sound, current medical information, not just, "because I said so." If you can't bring yourself to get the schools to do it, you better make sure you do it properly yourself, as a parent. The fact is, students exposed to real world sex education "abstain," that is, start having sex later than those taught abstinence only. Period. (3)

How did I come to this realization? I teach in a middle-upper class school district. Kids talk, both directly to me and to their peers within my earshot. Along with school counselors and psychologists, we deal with the middle school social and sexual drama daily.

One of the singular joys—and sometimes one of the terrors—of being a middle school science teacher in my school district is that the science department teaches the sex education curriculum. For a few weeks every year, I have a direct connection to that deeply revealing chatter as it pertains to the subject that looms large (and, it seems, ever larger in our culture) in all teenagers' lives:

SEX

The sex education unit is taught during the last two weeks of the school year under the wonderfully reassuring euphemism of "Family Life Education." It's a good program designed to be honestly informative while encouraging abstinence. We try to approach it with an open attitude and to tell our students, "This is the all the stuff you've heard about. We will answer all your questions. But until and unless you are able to take *responsibility* for birth control and STD (sexually transmitted disease) prevention as well as for what you will do if something goes wrong and you get pregnant or catch a disease anyway, you've got no business having sex." A lot of smart, conscientious kids will actively seek to prevent pregnancy and disease, but the second part of the equation (thinking about and knowing what you will do when it goes wrong) catches them completely off-guard. They are sophisticated yet sheltered, and they have a teenager's assumption that nothing bad will ever happen to them, and, if it does, there will be a pill or a parent to fix it so that there will be no real consequences—let alone permanent, life-altering ones—from their actions.

Much of the discussion in class, then, goes to showing them that, as 12 to 14 year olds, they are not in fact ready for these sexual responsibilities, any more than they are ready to drive or to drink responsibly. Or to put it another way, we try to show them that **there is nothing wrong or immature with saying, "I don't need or want this much responsibility at this point in my life. I'm going to put off sex until I can deal with this."** We consider it not a "how-to-do-it" class, but a "what-is-it" class. Surprisingly, a lot of the class hits home more than you might think. Being teenagers, many students consider themselves invulnerable, and they quickly come to learn about some of the trickier realities of sex.

"You mean, condoms break?!"

"You mean, if I miss a day of taking the pill, I could get pregnant?!"

"You mean, boys sometimes lie to get sex??"

"You mean, girls aren't always honest about birth control?"

"You mean, I could have an STD and not know about it for years?"

Being teenagers, much of the message will no doubt be lost ten minutes later, let alone in the heat of teen passion, but I think we improve the odds and delay the inevitable until they are at least a bit more self-aware and responsible.

One feature of our sex ed program is the universally loved question box, the source of the sample questions that opened this introduction, and the origin of much of what follows in this volume. The idea of the question box is that there are a lot of things kids are dying to know about sex that very few of them will raise their hand and ask about out loud. So we take an old shoe box, decorate it to suit (mine is an old CROCs box, decorated as the TMI—"Too Much Information"—Box) and place it on a desk or countertop with a stack of small slips of lined paper for the students to write their questions on. This is how they appear:

Question: _____

_____

_____

_____

_____

_____

Have you discussed this question with your parents?
Yes_____ No_____

Note that at the bottom of the slip, it asks, "Have you discussed this question with your parents?" with a yes/no check-off line. As one might guess, if it's checked at all, it's checked "no" 95 percent of the time. The question box fills rapidly, especially during the first days of the "Family Life" unit, as students feverishly write down question after question about every rumor, sexual urban legend, and random gross-out item they picked up on some adult web site their parents hadn't yet blocked. Usually, the last 10 or so minutes of the period are spent with the teacher answering question box questions, and the class usually becomes a sexual myths debunking session. Much of the real nature of sexual relationships and the debunking of the nonsense that "everyone knows" takes place in these sessions. Even the lamest of questions, often asked just to see if the asker (invariably a boy quivering with anticipation) can get away with it, can be rephrased to give pause and remind the class that sex involves not just instant gratification but also potential consequences for not one but many people – after the laughter from the contorted phrasing and tortured spelling subsides.

For me, the "Family Life Education" unit is a fascinating, wonderful slice of teenage life and humanity. When people sincerely ask how I can face teaching it, my reply is that, aside from believing in its real value, the unit is two weeks of sore stomach muscles as I try to keep from laughing out loud at the questions, or from losing that battle and laughing along with the students. Most of us who love middle school teaching (and many teachers understandably avoid teaching this chaotic period in student's lives) feel it's the last chance the teacher has to really influence who a student is and becomes, and nowhere is this more visible than in sex ed. Middle school teachers see elementary school kids as wonderfully moldable, but whiny and clingy. By high school, we feel that students are pretty much who they are going to be, and they have to make the decisions about their life with the guidance of great teachers and parents. In middle school, the kids are in this frightful, amazing explosion of maturing intelligence, growth, and hormones as they transition from little kids into virtual adults (this is especially true for many of the girls; guys catch up a few years later) where there are still infinite possibilities for the direction their life can take. Middle school teachers get to direct and shape this time in a boy/man/girl/woman's life.

In the end, this is a book about the questions we get asked as we try to influence, educate, and give positive direction to these amazing young lives during this harrowing time of transition. What follows is a compilation of the question box slips I've pulled over three years. These are standard questions from a normal range of kids, neither more or less sophisticated than I've encountered in the last several years. I've organized them into the following topics, more or less in the order of the interest that I see each year:

- ***Parts, Plumbing, and Puberty**, including questions about sizes, names, and terms they've heard and how the various parts of the sexual anatomy work.*
- **Masturbation**
- **Conception, Contraception, and Birth**
- **Sexually Transmitted Diseases and Infections (STDs and STIs)**
- ***Various Sex Acts**, including the increasingly popular fascination with:*
- **Anal (or Butt)Sex**
- **Sexuality**
- **All the Other Strange, Freaky, and Sometimes Sad Stuff They Ask About**
- **Sexual Harassment and Sexual Assault**
- **And Then, Some Questions Just Stand Alone...**

I will discuss each question in the following format:

- *The question, as written (often half the fun). I've printed the question in **boldface italics** to indicate that it is printed as worded, so I don't have to indicate with the tedious (sic) that the spelling, punctuation (or lack thereof), and grammar are exactly as written on the slip.*
- *How I rephrased it, if necessary.*
- *How I answered it to the class (and in some cases, how I wished I had answered it in class. This is a book—I get do-overs on what were extemporaneous remarks, however proud I was of them at the time.)*
- *The answer my inner smart ass middle school teacher/parent would have given if I wasn't a public school teacher and valued my job.*
- *Further, in-depth discussion of a topic as needed in asides directed to the reader, supplementing my verbal response to the students.*

You may notice that I sometimes answer the same, or virtually the same, question in different sections, depending on the context. This is intentional, both to address the differing context and because middle schoolers benefit from repetition.

So, I hope you enjoy what follows as much as I enjoyed reading, teaching, researching, and writing about it. You have amazing kids, but what they know, or think they know, is way beyond the world most of their parents and grandparents grew up in.

Please note that this is the first, uploaded on-line edition of this book. Future editions will have photo reproductions of the actual slips (I have **all of them** safely at home), plus whatever new, amazing stuff the kids ask me until then.

Finally, before we begin, a bit about Fran and me. I was born in 1950 in Long Beach, California, where I still live. I'm a classic

Baby Boomer: child of the 50's, grew up in the 60's, did some scary stuff in the 70's, then got married and had two daughters in the 80's. I have a journalism BA, and an Engineering BS from California State University, Long Beach. I worked at a local newspaper, then for some years in my family's sailboat hardware manufacturing business, then spent nearly 20 years in the aerospace materials industry. I made the best career move of my life, getting into teaching, when aerospace contracted sharply in the early '90s, picking up my first teaching credential at Cal State Dominguez and a Master's degree in school administration from Pepperdine. I've been married to the same amazing woman, Frannie Spokane, since 1977. She is a practicing speech pathologist, and she taught me almost everything I know about how young people's brains work and develop, information that is unconscionably rare in many teaching curriculums across the country. That my two beautiful grown daughters, Natasha and Nicole, turned out to be the amazing young women that they are is largely due to her effort and wisdom.

Fran is a Pittsburgh native, transplanted to southern California in her early 20's. She grew up in a small Pittsburgh neighborhood, enjoying a rich education by way of advanced educational programs that used to be the norm in most school districts. She was a straight A student, always hard working. She was a creative force throughout her school years, singing, writing plays, performing in local theatre, and dreaming of a "life on Broadway". She came to her senses, and pursed her higher education experience, by going to Pennsylvania State University, University of Pittsburgh, and when she moved to California, finished her Bachelors Degree and Masters Degree in Communicative Disorders at California State University, Long Beach. She has been a practicing Speech-Language Pathologist both in the schools and privately to the present. She has also taught part time at the college level. She has worked with all age groups throughout her career and often does trainings for parents in the local school district to support communication skills.

I (Dave) make no claim to be a professional sex educator beyond the fact that I have taken the excellent training on sex education in my school district (as well as being a member of the committee responsible for updating the district's curriculum) and the experience of living with three women for decades. I'm a reasonably intelligent, concerned parent and educator. As I explain to my students at the start of Family Life Education, "I realize that a middle age man is probably the last person you, especially young women, would want to hear about this subject from. However, there is *nothing* that you are going through growing to adulthood that I haven't been through myself and/or with the women in my life. I've bought bales of tampons (three different brands because, of course, each woman had her own preference) with a straight face and without embarrassment. I've picked up any number of prescriptions for birth control pills, as well as medications for various and sundry aliments that occur "down there." I've had to leave work to pick up a daughter incapacitated in the school nurse's office with the monumental cramps of her early periods. I've had an ear on all the social drama of middle and high school, both as a parent and teacher. As much as any man can, I get what it's like to be that age, certainly as a male (my daughters say the longer I teach middle school, the more I act that age – my wife says I always have), and as a father of daughters." As you will see in the latter part of this book, I have a lot more to say on this subject following the questions and answers shared below.

With that honest disclaimer, here goes...

PARTS, PLUMBING, AND PUBERTY

SIZE QUESTIONS!

One thing that is difficult to keep in mind as a teacher is the vast, schizophrenic gulf in what middle school students do and don't know. Some can look like frightfully mature college co-eds, while others can appear physically unchanged since third grade. Some are sexually active and have tried most of the things seen in your average porn production (yes, really) yet still believe that if a girl is on top during sex she can't get pregnant. Others are truly in the dark and don't know the most basic terms and concepts like "ovary" and "menstruation." Really. Most fall in between, knowing as much or more than they want, but still filled with uncertainty, curiosity, and confusion, hovering between, "OMG, leave me alone, I don't even want to deal with this now" and "But what happens if I let him (insert various sex acts or concerns here....)?" By far the vast majority are at least technically virgins, having not had penetrative sex, and really not much of any other kind of sex either. Between their actual inexperience, the conflicting sexual images and practices seen in the media, and the constantly evolving street slang for everything sexual, it's hardly surprising that there are huge amounts of confusion as to what is what, what it's called, and how big it or they should be. Many of the questions are simply "what is?.." or "how big is?.." questions. You don't have to be a guy to guess what the vast majority of size questions relate to.

Question: How big can a penis get?
How long can a penis grow?
Does size matter?
What if your penis is too small?
How big is your penis suppose to be when your 14?

My answer: Ah, the perennial question, central to the lives of all human males. First, how big? Multiple statistical studies have shown that the ***average adult male erect penis is 5 and 1/2 to just under 6 inches long***. You measure from base of the penis on top to the tip when erect (you can see the boys eyes glaze over as they try to remember where the rulers or tape measures are at home). Most of you are still growing, so it's going to change. There is virtually no connection between the flaccid (non-erect) length and the erect length, so comparisons between yourself and the other guys in gym class are pointless. Penises that look small flaccid can be big when erect and vice versa. The largest reliably measured erect penis (that is, measured by a qualified doctor in a real scientific study) was 13.5 inches long. If it helps your self-image, the average human male has a penis far bigger than a chimpanzee's or even a 600 pound adult male gorilla's.(3)

Does size matter? Short answer *(ha!)*: it depends. Like everything else, everyone has preferences and individual likes and dislikes based on how they are built and, more importantly, what their own preference is in their own mind. Never forget that the brain is the main sex organ, not the equipment between your legs. Physiologically, the size of the penis should make no difference in sexually satisfying and/or impregnating a partner. Many studies of female preferences show that while there is a definite minority of women who prefer a large penis ("large" not being defined here), the vast majority of women just don't care and/or find intercourse with a man with a large penis uncomfortable or painful. Most women think men worry about it way too much compared to the small importance it has to women. If they have a preference at all, most women prefer a thicker penis to a longer one in terms of sexual satisfaction, probably because it stimulates the outer part of the vagina and clitoris more. Again remember, that the main sex organ is the brain. What we want and desire and need sexually starts there. Penis preferences have more to do with what people think they want than what actually matters physically.

What you also have to remember is that all the nerves that provide stimulation to a woman during intercourse are in the clitoris, around the opening of the vagina and in the outer couple inches or so of the vagina. The upper part of the vagina near the cervix has virtually no nerves, so the penis reaching up there does little anyway. If the penis is large or long enough to hit the cervix during intercourse, that *can* cause pain there and in the uterus. (4, 5)

At 14, almost all guys are still growing to some extent, and your penis will continue to grow with you, though probably not as much as you would like.

Question: Is it possible for a penis not to fit in a vagina?

Answer: Normal, healthy adults should be able to insert pretty much any penis into any vagina. They are just not that different in size, and, again, if a woman can pass a baby through her vagina, a penis really is no big deal. If there is a big size difference between the two people, they may have to proceed with some care, but, given that, there should be no problem. By care, I mean thoughtful consideration of the woman involved, making sure she is aroused, relaxed, and lubricated. Forceful penetration, before the woman is ready, can be a whole different situation, and unless the guy is a complete tool or a rapist, he will remember that.

Now, if the girl is young, inexperienced, or a virgin, then it could be very difficult for her to accept a large penis, though again, patience and care can overcome a lot.

Question: What is "hung" and what is cum? Why have I been told that girls like men hung like a horse?

Answer: "Hung" is a slang term referring to the size of a guy's penis. "Hung like a horse" means you've got a big one, like a horse supposedly. Most guys would prefer not to be described as "hung like a hamster." As discussed above, most women do not in fact want to have sex with a horse-size penis, the "hung" thing being largely a guy obsession.

"Cum" can be a verb or a noun. As a verb, "to cum" is slang for an orgasm, either female or male. The noun "cum" refers to the actual ejaculate or semen produced by a male orgasm or ejaculation.

Question: What is jizz?

Answer: Jizz is more or less synonymous with cum, except that it is a male reference only. "Jizz" the verb refers to ejaculation, while "jizz" the noun describes semen.

Question: Is a black man's penis bigger than a white man's?

Is it true that African American's have larger penis than other races?
Why do black guys usually have bigger wieners???
Why are black people penises so much bigger?
Is it true that Asians have small penises?

My answer: This is tricky and obviously a sensitive subject, but we do have scientific data! The short answer is that this too is a myth. Again, multiple studies by scientists working for condom manufacturers (who have to get this size thing right!) have shown that there is no statistical difference in penis size between the races. To put it another way, there are bigger differences in size among guys in the same race than there are differences in penis size between the races. Now, some common sense here: if you are in a locker room with a bunch of near seven foot tall NBA players or NFL linebackers of *any race,* these are huge guys, and their penises are going to be on average larger than the average guy's penis. If most of them are African American, it's going to be hard not to think that black dudes have big penises. But we are talking about overall average sizes, and not all black people are giant athletes. The same thing applies if you are in a locker room with a bunch of Asian gymnasts who are in a sport where it pays to be small and lean (let's face it, Dwight Howard and Lebron aren't going to shine on the parallel bars or floor exercises), you are not going to see a lot of huge penises. But most Asian people are not little wiry gymnasts. If you are in northern China and Korea, there are some *big* (Yao Ming!) Asian dudes with penises to match! Averages, people!

Question: Are different types of race (girls) tighter than others?

Answer: Seriously?? No. See above.

Question: How far can a penis go up a vagina? How deep is a vagina?

Answer: (*Note that this is still a "size" question, usually, but not always, from a worried guy. Aside from wanting to know if their penis is big enough to be studly and proud of, many guys are sincerely worried about hurting a girl when they do eventually have sex. Both boys and girls are often deeply suspicious that "there is no way that thing will fit in there."*)

For some reason, many young people view the vagina as some cavernous, bottomless tunnel. It's not. The vagina is typically about four or so inches deep and a bit deeper when sexually aroused. Amazingly, the average erect penis and the average *aroused* vagina are virtually the same length and depth: about six inches for the penis, slightly shorter for the vagina. How about that?! But there is so much more to sex than inches. Keep in mind that the vagina stretches to pass a baby, so your penis is not as big a challenge as you might hope.

Question: Can a girl flex her vagina like a guy flexes his penis?
Does the girl get anything with their vagina like a boy get an erection?

Answer: Remember, the vagina is a set of muscles that a woman actually has considerable control over. She can contract or squeeze her vagina and relax it. With practice she can do that in a variety of ways. Guys have limited control over their penis because it is not a muscle in itself. An erection is the result of a reflex action of the muscles around certain blood vessels that exit the penis that a man has limited, if any, control over.

Now, girls do experience things in their vagina/vulva that are reflexive actions, similar to a man's erection when they are aroused sexually. The first of those reflexes is that the vaginal walls lubricate so that the vagina is ready for penetration. Girls feel this as "getting wet" down there when they are sexually aroused. As arousal continues, the clitoris gets its own little mini-erection, becoming harder while the tip pokes out a little from under its hood of skin. The labia around the vulva get a bit fatter as they engorge with blood and the vagina lengthens. None of these things are visually obvious the way an erection is on a guy, but girls and women are certainly aware of them.

Question: If you ejaculate more, will your penis be bigger? (The size obsession again.) Is it true that if you masterbate your penius gets smaller? (like I say, the spelling is half the fun!)

My Answer: Nope, sorry, no connection. Your penis size is what you are born with, like any other part of your body. Most of you guys are still growing, and you can expect your penis to grow some yet as well. But that's it. If ejaculating a lot made your penis grow or shrink, most teenage boys would have terrifyingly large penises being pushed around in wheel barrows—or no penis at all.

Question: Is it true that if your shoe size (hand size, hat size, etc.) is big your penis is big?

My Answer: Shoe size, penis size, and all the other sizes of our body parts range from small to large, with the great majority of us in some middle, average range. I know of no scientifically verified studies that link shoe size to penis size. In fact, a recent study in England proved pretty conclusively that there is no connection. Logically, big guys are going to, on average, have big feet and big penises. Most of us would feel small if we had had to shower next to Shaquille O'Neal after an NBA game. Beyond that, there is not much to choose, and a five foot 10 man with size 15 shoes is not necessarily going to have a big penis. (4, 5, 6)

Question: Girls have three holes?!?!
Do girls have two holes in their vagina?
How many holes do girls have?

Answer: *(Note to reader: This could refer to a couple of related questions. The person either wants confirmation that the mouth, vagina, and anus are available for sex, or has just gotten wind of the fact that the girl's urethra is separate from the vagina, the anus still being a third hole.)* Unlike men, a woman's urethra (the pee hole) is separate from the sexual passage, the vagina. In men, urine and semen pass through the same tube. In women, they are separate, primarily for the obvious reason that the vagina has to pass a baby, whereas in men, the urethral tube only has to pass urine and semen. As to the third hole, people are usually referring either to the mouth or the anus, and we all have both of those. Women's plumbing tends to be more specialized, whereas the male anatomy tends to multitask.

Question: What in the world is a chode. I'm so confused? (Spellings vary widely, with chode, choda, and other guesses common. Various terms come into vogue and are subjects of intense interest from year to year. This was the year of the chode.)

My Answer: This is one of those terms whose street meaning and definition changes almost minute by minute. Despite what you've heard, the current generally accepted definition as noted on the websites of "Talk Sex" host nurse Sue Johanson and the Urban Dictionary.com (an invaluable resource when trying to keep up with street slang) is that this is what often used to be called the "taint," or the wrinkly brown skin between the scrotum (ball sack) and the anus.

What my inner smart ass wanted to say: Actually, it's a good general term for about a third of any randomly selected sample of middle school boys. Many of us go through the phase and grow out of it.

Question: How come I wake up every morning with a really stiff boner?

Answer: Because you're a dude! Be proud! This is an almost universal experience for all males. An erection is a reflex of nerves and muscles, like sneezing or kicking your lower leg when the doctor taps just below your knee. It's not always connected with sex or sexual arousal. Think how many times you have found yourself with an erection when you were not in fact thinking about sex. It can be brought on by any number of random stimuli, including needing to go to the bathroom, as most of us need to do rather urgently upon waking in the morning. Of course, the erection can make that kind of tricky.

Question: What does it mean if your penis is crooked?

Answer: Unless your penis has had a serious injury, it just means that it's crooked, period. It's like having a slightly crooked nose or any of our other parts that aren't perfectly symmetrical. As long as you can pee normally, ejaculate normally, and get erections normally, a crooked penis is of no concern.

Question: What happens if my penis snaps? When your humping and you go out too far and come out, then if you try to go back in, but miss could the penis break if you push hard enough? (The natural bloodthirstiness of middle school boys makes it inevitable that you get a lot of "what if?" questions about injuries, however unlikely.)

Answer: It is possible for the penis to be injured or "broken," which is something to remember the next time you want to imitate your heroes on "Jackass." Remember, the penis doesn't really have a bone in it (unlike dogs, seals, cats, and most carnivorous animals, which do in fact have a penis bone). However, the erect penis can be over-bent and "broken." If the erect or flaccid penis is injured, it can bleed a lot (remember, it's full of spongy tissue and LOTS of blood vessels), require surgery, and form scar tissue, all of which HURTS! Modern surgery techniques can do an amazing job of repairing severe injuries. However, people have lost parts of their penis to injury, and others have ended up with crooked and improperly functioning penises. Males don't have a strong instinct to protect that area for nothing. (7)

Question: Is it possible to pop your balls by squeezing it?

How come when you get hit in the balls it hurts so much?

Answer: Ah, a question only a middle school guy could ask. Of course! If you squeeze your testicle hard enough it will rupture or pop. Now, to prevent middle school guys from testing this, we have evolved pain nerves in that area sensitive enough that you will stop squeezing well before you do any damage. Otherwise middle school age guys would all have to try and see if they could squeeze and pop their balls, and if it worked on one testicle, they'd have to pop the other one and take a picture with their cell phone just to show their friends how cool it was! So, we'd have a bunch of sterile (but cool!) guys who never could father kids, and we'd go extinct in one generation. Your testicles aren't called "the family jewels" for nothing. The sperm that allows your (questionable) genes to be passed on to future generations is made there. The excruciating pain of testicle abuse makes sure you take good care of them.

Question: If you get an orgasim can your penis like blow up or splode from too much like blood and spurm going to the penis? (Along with the "Cameltoe?" question below, this was my favorite of that year.)

Answer: No, that won't happen. Again, this is one of those wise evolutionary adaptations. All the guys whose penises exploded from too much sperm and blood going to their penis either died or found it hard to get dates, get married, or father children. So only those guys whose penises did *not* explode fathered children, and they passed their non-explosive penis genes down through the generations to you, so that you don't have to worry about it.

However, the gene for spelling ability does not seem to be connected with this.

Question: What is skeet?

Answer: It is, in my experience, a relatively recent slang term for semen.

Question: Why is semen clear/misty-grey sometimes & watery white other times semen is white & thick? (This kid asked a lot of thoughtful, observant questions that indicated both intelligence and more experience than perhaps a 14 year old boy needs to have.)

Answer: Seminal fluid varies mostly due to how hydrated a man is. That is, if you have had a lot of liquids, your semen will tend to be more watery, whereas if you're dehydrated it will be thicker. Color varies because people vary, period, in their genetics, diet, and other factors that influence body fluids.

Question: How many penises can u fit in a girl's vagina?
I don't get how 2 penises can fit into 1 vagina. (Ah, text speak! These kids clearly got on websites they shouldn't have, or into a college age brother's porn stash. Note that subtly, this is another size question. Depending on the group of kids and what I know of the outlook of their parents, this might

be one of the rare questions I would pass on answering. In this case, I went for it.)

My Answer: Looks like I'm going to have to again warn parents about maintaining their porn site blocking software... Look, multiple partner sex can be risky, and that's what you are talking about here. Keep in mind that when you have sex, especially unprotected sex, with anyone, you are having sex with *everyone else* those people have had sex with. You are exposed to all the STDs those people have been exposed to. Even if both guys wear condoms, there is a greater chance of one or more of them breaking from the two penises and condoms rubbing against each other *(Note to reader: this inevitably elicits giggles, followed by terrified cries of teenage homophobic horror)* – or some other form of Murphy's Law coming into play. Now assuming that some woman had the bad taste to have sex with more than one of any of you, remember that the vagina can pass a baby, so if she is so inclined, more than one penis could probably be accommodated. However, there are so many potential bad outcomes to this experimentation at your age that it's probably a bad idea all around...

Question: What does a vagina look like?

Answer: A picture (groans from the kids - they want pictures, but sexual anatomy graphics deeply embarrass many of them) is worth a thousand words. Again, when people say vagina, they usually mean the vulva, a woman's externally visible sex organs. This overhead slide gives a rather plain medical view. A guy can also stand in front of a mirror, tuck your penis and scrotum back behind your legs and get a pretty good idea of what a woman sees when she looks in the mirror.

Question: Does it always hurt when a girl loses her virginity?
Why does it hurt the first time for a girl?

Answer: No, not always. Like most things in life, girls experience their first sexual intercourse in many different ways. But, like the doctor says when he's about to administer a shot or some medical test, there is often "discomfort."

Physically, most virgin girls have a small membrane called a hymen that partially covers the opening of the vagina. The actual function of the hymen is an open question. All women are born with one, and they vary, like all the other parts of our bodies do from person to person. Some hymens are hardly there at all, and a few almost totally close the vagina and have to be cut in a minor surgery at the gynecologist's office. During a woman's first sexual intercourse, it is common for the hymen to be stretched and torn, causing some pain and bleeding. On the other hand, many girls/women have their first intercourse without pain or bleeding, either because their hymen doesn't present that much of an obstacle or because it's already been stretched or torn accidentally or without the girl's knowledge during sports or other activities. My wife's was broken when she did a hard sit-down fall water skiing as a teen. There was some pain (which she attributed to the fall) and slight bleeding, with no sex involved at all. Even though her hymen had been broken, it still hurt a bit the first few times she had sex. In other words, pain and bleeding during your first sexual intercourse is a very unreliable indication of virginity, despite all the cultural importance some people attach to the process.

The other thing to remember is that the vagina is a set of muscles. As a virgin, a girl's vagina muscles are not used to the normal stretching and contractions of sex, and this first encounter with the bulk of a penis can hurt the way any under-used muscle can hurt when you first stretch and exercise it. Further, if the girl is nervous or scared or embarrassed, as almost all of us are to some extent the first time we have sex, this can make the muscles of her vagina tense, adding to the discomfort. So "the first time" is often not that great for girls because usually she and the boy she is with don't really know what they are doing, and the patience, gentleness, and care needed to make it easier just aren't there. The first intercourse, like most things in life, is different for everyone. Some girls will have no problem, most won't enjoy it all that much, and for some, it will be pretty unpleasant. Most everybody finds it gets better with time and practice, like learning any other new skill. We do know that starting later than the middle school years is emotionally and psychologically better and physically easier for women. That may sound like just another thing grown-ups tell you to keep you under control, but if you think at all about it, it's common sense. You do much better at most things when you are more mature and ready for them. (8)

Question: What is a camal toe?
Cameltoe? (This may be the most succinct question I've ever been asked. Cameltoe was right in there with chode as the term of choice for one year.)

Answer: First, you have to know that camel feet have two padded toes, such that, when you look at the bottom of a camel's foot, it looks remarkably like the female human's vulva or external sex organs. So, when a woman wears pants, workout clothes, or a bathing suit bottom that's way too tight and fitted, it tends to outline the vulva so that it looks like a "cameltoe." This is truer in this era when many women – but by no means all – completely shave their pubic hair. Guys of course love cameltoes, while women consider it a major fashion faux pas.

The question: Are black women's vaginas really purple?

Answer: Yes, and so are many white women's. First, let's get some terminology straight. The *vagina* is the muscular canal or tube between the uterus and cervix and the outside of a woman's body. The *vulva* is the proper term for the woman's external sex organs, what you see when a girl looks at herself naked in the mirror. Unless you're a gynecologist with the proper tools, you can't see the vagina from the outside, only the vulva. The vulva includes the labia or vaginal lips, the outer end of the clitoris, the urethral and vaginal opening, and whatever pubic hair the woman has allowed to remain in the area. People commonly say vagina when what they really mean is the vulva.

So, back to color: the tissues of the vulva and vagina are somewhat erectile, like the penis, but not quite as much. That means that when these areas are sexually aroused, they get pumped up and swollen with blood. This, as you might expect on such thin skinned tissues, influences their color, and, when aroused, the vulva can be a deep purply pink. As a woman matures, and particularly if she has given birth vaginally, the coloring effect is more intense, and her aroused vulva can be almost purple, whether she is white or black. The outer vulva skin and labia are pigmented, obviously more so in African American women and other women of color, and this can enhance and darken the effect. The inner vulva tissues of any race are not pigmented. Inside the labia, all women are pink.

Question: Why is the color of my penis darker than my upper thighs. I never tan naked.

Answer: Very much as we were discussing above with regard to women, the pigmentation and skin color of the sex organs in men tends to be darker than the rest of their skin. If you are a red head with little pigmentation, you skin down there still tends to be a darker pink. If you have any skin color at all, the penis and scrotum are noticeably darker than the rest of your skin, even if they have never seen sunlight. Again, this is likely an evolutionary adaptation to protect these delicate, thin-skinned, and valuable organs from sun damage when we were creatures that spent our lives naked in the sunlight.

Question: Can a woman's breasts be flattened permanently?

Answer: I'm not sure what we are going for here. Breasts are mostly fat tissue. The glands and ducts that produce milk don't take up much room, and flat chested women can nurse just as well as large breasted women. Since they are made of fat, they can't be popped or ruptured in the way the questioner is probably thinking. Of course they can be injured in accidents like any other part of your body. Over a woman's life they will tend to change shape and sag a bit lower due to the effects of gravity, especially if not properly supported by bras. If a woman nurses, they can change shape some after she is done nursing, but not always. If the woman has had breast implants, these are plastic bags filled with saline water or silicone gel. It is possible for these to be damaged and ruptured, which will obviously change their shape.

Question: How come guys don't get boobs?

Answer: Well, guys don't need to feed/nurse babies, unlike women and all female mammals. Remember, the term "mammals" has the root word *mammary*, which is the scientific term for breasts and the milk production glands, or mammary glands. This is one of the key things that define mammals. No other group of animals on this planet has this equipment. You've probably noticed that men have nipples, which is because nature and evolution uses the same basic structures for both sexes as needed. Men don't develop the milk-producing glands women do, but they can sometimes, at this point in life when your hormones are in a jumble, produce a little of the fluid that women produce in pregnancy before they make milk. It's not common, it's temporary, and it's no big deal.

The fact is, many evolutionary scientists think that breasts have the shape and bulk they do as a sexual signal to men. They don't need to be that size and shape to nurse. Few mammals, including our close relatives the chimpanzees and gorillas, have anything as bulky as human breasts, and flat chested women nurse babies with no problems. So it's pretty logical that the primitive hominid females with bigger breasts attracted more male (male hominids were apparently into visual stimulation just like modern guys) attention and produced more babies than those that didn't have large breasts. The breast-growing genes got passed on so that humans generally have bigger breasts than needed for anything but attracting male attention. Like I said, this all sounds pretty logical given what we know about breasts and evolution, but given that these evolutionary decisions were made hundreds of thousands of years ago, it is pretty hard to get actual scientific data to support any particular hypothesis. (9, 10, 11)

Question: What is a clit?

Answer: First, you have to understand that, as noted above, males and females are all made from the same basic hardware, evolutionarily rearranged and adjusted to suit. When you were tiny little fetuses inside your mom, both boys and girls looked pretty much like girls down there. Your gonads (the organs that become either testes or ovaries) were up inside your body like the ovaries are in girls, and the external stuff, what there was at all, looked pretty much like girls.

If your chromosomes said you're a guy, then the hormones that make you a guy start being released by your glands and told the body, "dude, you're a guy." So the gonads moved down inside the body and outside into the little baby scrotum and became sperm-making testes or testicles (same thing). The tissue that becomes the penis grew out around the urethra (the pee tube) and became your penis.

In girl fetuses, the female hormones told the gonads to stay where they were, became ovaries, and started forming all the little egg cells that a woman will release later in life. The tissue that becomes a penis in men stayed mostly inside her body (about four inches of it), with just the little button end sticking out just above the urethra opening in the vulva. (9) This is the *clitoris*, or "clit" for short. It is made out of erectile tissue like the penis, and it even gets its own mini-erection when aroused, though only the very tip of it can be felt or seen outside the body. The clitoris is loaded with sensitive nerve cells, which are much more densely packed than those of the penis. In fact, the clitoris has more nerves for its size than any tissue in men's or women's bodies—and it is the center of sexual sensation and arousal for women, just like the penis is for men. The fact is, sexual stimulation is the ONLY purpose of the clitoris. *(The realization that the clitoris is the main thing for women, not the vagina or the action of the man's penis, is always tough on guys, until one sees the implications of this realization dawn in the faces of the very few perceptive ones.)* (12)

Author's note to the reader: One startling realization for me as a teacher is that even in my upscale neighborhood in this sexualized, over-informed age, is that fully half the girls in 8th grade do not seem to realize they have a clitoris, or if they do, they are fuzzy at best about its function in their life. On the other hand, they just may be very good at acting surprised and ladylike when the subject is broached so they aren't perceived as slutty, because heaven forbid anyone find out they masturbate.

So, whether it's an act or real ignorance stemming from the age-old, almost instinctive fear of women's sexuality and what girls might do when they find out about this part of their body, or if it's simply one of those things that gets left out of discussions of tampons and periods, I don't know. I'll come back to this in the discussion of masturbation questions later.

Question: How come guys have penises and girls have vaginas? Why isn't it the other way around?

Answer: Well, your question is really about the names we give things, isn't it? Scientists have recently discovered fossils of prehistoric fish from 375 million years ago (way before the dinosaurs) that appear to be the first creatures with penis and uterus organs. These fossils even contain baby fish fetus fossils with an umbilical cord attaching them to their mother within the mother fish's fossil. This extinct group of fish, called Placoderms, is probably related to the ancestors of modern shark-like fish, who have the same double penis, double uterus equipment that we see in these ancient fossils. Other fish have evolved different internal fertilization organs, while most lizards and snakes have the same set-up as these ancient fish, with double penises and uteruses. Mammals evolved single penises and uteruses. That's the way evolution worked on our planet.

The purpose of sex from an evolutionary standpoint is to allow gene mixing, because that gives offspring more genetic evolutionary options than creatures who just divide and produce exact copies of themselves, like many single celled creatures still do. However, even bacteria started hooking up and exchanging genetic DNA material billions of years ago, and as creatures became larger and more complex, it became an evolutionary advantage to protect and nurture the reproductive cells, sperm and eggs, in the body of the adult. Since the sex we eventually called "female" produced the larger egg cell, and later the still larger, shelled eggs, and still later, the shell-less embryos of sharks and some reptiles, it was a safer, evolutionary advantage (that is, more babies from such mothers survived and had offspring of their own with the same genes) to transfer the small, numerous sperm cells into the female to fertilize these large eggs there, rather than haphazardly fertilizing them externally like most fish and amphibians still do. The Placoderm fish evolved organs to do this in the form of flesh covered bony extensions of their pelvic bones (yes, they really *do* have boners) that carried a tube to transfer sperm from the male testis to the female's uterus during mating. We humans call this sex "male" today.

You have to remember, that the creatures that evolved these organs didn't have words or concepts in their minds about guys and girls. They didn't care since they were just trying to survive and reproduce. Humans came up with those names and our ideas about what guys and girls are or should be, hundreds of millions of years after these creatures just had sex because they needed to, and it worked better. We could have just as easily called guys girls, and girls guys or men, and it wouldn't matter if we all agreed on what the names were. (13)

> **Question:** What is that very distinct smell coming out of my vagina? It smells like fish.
> Why does vagina smell like fish?
> What does vagina taste like?
> Why does a womens vagina smell like sushi? No offense to Asians

Answer: Actually, a normal, healthy vagina itself doesn't have much of a smell or taste itself. What you smell is the normal discharge from the vagina drying and being acted on by common bacteria in your underwear and, to some extent, in your pubic hair. Some of the chemicals produced as byproducts are similar to the chemicals that produce the smell of fish. However, if there is a *strong* fishy smell, accompanied by yellowish, greenish, or foamy-appearing discharge, this can mean an infection by single-celled protozoan germs like Trichomonas or Gardnerella. These infections are generally easily treated, but you need to get to a gynecologist and get them looked after.

As to taste, it's like chicken....

Question: What's a cunt? What's a queef? (Both questions on the same earnest girl's question slip.)
If my boyfriend eats me out, how can I prevent from queefing?
What is a queef?

Answer: The "C" word is right up there with the "F" word in being unacceptable in polite or school discussion (I don't say either word, ever, in Family Life discussions). It's just a very old English word – at least a 1000 years old or more – for the vulva/vagina.

Now a queef is just a fun little word for a vaginal fart. Air can get trapped in the vagina, not necessarily in connection with sex. When it is released or squeezed out by vaginal muscle contractions, it can make a little fart noise. I don't know that any one has worried enough about it to actually develop preventive measures. Even if it's a bit embarrassing, it's funny enough that both people usually laugh it off and that's it.

Expanded discussion for the reader: How did *I* learn (or rather, re-learn) what a queef was? Let me tell the story as an aside, just to give an indication of the sexually fearless nature of some of the young ladies one encounters in middle school these days. This, of course, is a story I never share in school with students. A few years ago I was supervising the disciplinary institution called "Saturday School," the Saturday morning detention for the seriously clueless and/or harder core bad actors on campus. As one would expect, it runs 80% or more boys, but there are girls that make regular appearances, usually for repeated violations of dress code, academic cheating, and/or gum chewing. This particular morning, I was preoccupied grading papers at my desk as the kids did their time, when one little troublesome 7th grade hottie giggled quietly. I looked up with the appropriate stern expression to see that she was looking at me with a surprised but very pleased smile on her face.

"Mr. Beck, guess what? I just made a queef!"

Luckily, this Saturday there was only one other girl there (who looked horrified), and a brain dead slacker in the far corner of the room who hadn't picked up on the conversation, so I didn't face the chaotic hilarity that might normally have resulted from such a statement in the presence of a dozen or so middle school tools. At that time, I truly hadn't a clue as to what she was talking about, and, being preoccupied with my grading, I innocently, distractedly, foolishly asked, "What's a queef?" thinking it referred to some doodle or middle school craft fad of the moment. How I reached my late 40's without registering the word queef, I don't know. My wife pointed out that we had joked about it at various times in our relationship, but it escaped my mind, deer-in-the-headlights fashion, here. Like lawyers, teachers learn to never ask a question if they don't already know the answer, and I ignored that wisdom to my peril.

"It's a fart you make with your vagina," she replied with a sprightly smile, delighted that she could share this fact with me in this disciplinary setting. "I can make them on purpose with my muscles! Wanna hear me?"

Now, I am famous for *never, ever* being at a loss for words or a zinger comeback to a kid's lame remark. Here, I was speechless.

Dumbfounded.

Silent.

For many seconds.

I *may* have avoided blushing – I don't recall. I finally managed to mumble something about the inappropriateness of the remark, that I wanted to hear no more about it, and that she risked at least one more Saturday school if she said anything of the kind again. The latter threat ended any further discussion, and I quietly spent the rest of the session trying to grade papers while the paranoid thoughts about the legal/career consequences of an inadvertent, inappropriate sexual discussion with a 13 year old fevered my mind....

Question: "Why do my nipples get hard?"

Answer: Nipples are "erectile tissue" like the penis and the tissues in the vulva and vagina. When suitably stimulated they engorge with blood, becoming harder and sticking out more. With nipples, this can happen as part of sexual arousal, but also in response to cold and/or general excitement from any source.

Question: Why is pubic hair thick and prickly? What is the point of pubic hair? Is it normal to not have any at 14?

Answer: If you look at animals, you may notice that in the area where we as humans have pubic hair, most animals have less or no hair. Or to put it another way, even though humans have little body hair, we have a lot of it in our pubic areas. Why?

Most anthropologists and evolutionary scientists believe that a combination of factors contributed to our pubic hair abundance. From a biomechanics standpoint, it actually appears to act as a chafe guard/lubricant in areas of our body that rub together as we move. That is, our armpits and the area between our thighs rub as we walk or run, moving our arms past our body and our legs past each other in ways that animals that walk on all fours don't. Pubic and armpit hair reduce the chafe that bare skin would experience in the hot, damp, tropical environments where we evolved. Many social scientists feel that since we are very visual, social, and sexual creatures, pubic hair is also a visual signal that calls attention to this area. The presence of a healthy bush of pubic hair indicates that the person is sexually mature and available. It also probably serves to hold the scents and pheromones that stimulate and attract people sexually. From a more practical standpoint, pubic hair no doubt serves to protect the important and delicate sex organs from dirt, sun, and other dangers and irritants. Remember, we evolved walking around naked and sitting on the bare ground on our bare butts. Because pubic hair serves this protective function, it must be robust, so the hairs are thicker, dense, and usually curly, even in straight haired people.

As to what's normal, that varies like everything else about people. At your age, it is perfectly normal to still have little or no pubic hair, though most people are starting to get some. If you haven't, you will, don't sweat it. When fully adult, some people have lots, some almost none, and everything in between—just like everything else about humans. (15)

Question: Is it bad to shave/wax down there? Is it better to have hair, or none at all?

Answer: There is really nothing good or bad about grooming pubic hair. It's a matter of style, fashion, and personal choice. First, understand that serious pubic hair grooming has come and gone through the centuries. You may think it's a current, hip, stylish thing to shave or groom your pubic hair, but, as every generation eventually discovers, they in fact didn't discover sex, and there really is nothing new in sexuality. In Europe and America pubic grooming has become a big thing again in last 10 years or so, and by no means exclusively for women. For much of human history a full pubic bush was considered normal and attractive for the reasons noted above. Besides, when most people are concerned with day to day survival, doing anything special the pubic bush is pretty low on the priority list. However, in much of the Islamic world, pubic and body hair removal has long been considered part of the quest for purity and cleanliness. On the other hand, many people of the Hindu faith practice the "Kush" tradition of never cutting or shaving *any* hair, anywhere on their body, feeling that God made them the way they are, and that's perfect as it is. Among the rich in Western culture, there have been pubic grooming fads over the centuries, going back at least to the ancient Egyptians. These fads have included shaving, brewing various questionable concoctions to remove pubic hair, or keeping the bush and braiding jewels and beads into the hair.

The pornography and exotic dancer industries have made pubic hair grooming or removal a big thing again, and many people spend a great deal of time and money grooming, trimming or removing all or part of their bush. Like every other grooming topic, it is a matter of personal preference and/or something done to please a lover/spouse. Personally, I find it amusing that young people can't wait to grow up, with the growth of pubic hair signaling "at last! I'm an adult!" Then they shave it all off so that they look like a six year old again.

As to styles, many people still love a full bush, while others are horrified by anything but complete hair removal. Frankly I'm amazed at the intensity of the arguments and attitudes toward these two sides of pubic grooming. Most people content themselves with shaving or removing part of their pubic hair, leaving and styling various amounts to suit. It's *your* pubic hair, so you pretty much get to do what you want with it (though Mom would probably like to have a say in the matter if you are going to use her razors, wax, or creams), but remember: just like guys find with shaving their face, once you start shaving, it's kind of an all or nothing thing. You have to keep at it or let it grow in. As always, keep clean and use good products.

While researching this, I tried to find any connection with pubic hair removal and vaginal health issues. There does not appear to be anything definite, but some gynecologists feel that women who remove their pubic hair have more vaginal and yeast infections. I don't know of any actual scientific study that links these issues, but there is logic to it. We evolved pubic hair to protect that area (see above). Removing that protection may well leave the vagina less protected and more subject to infection. Something to keep in mind.

Furthermore, the skin down there is delicate, and shaving or waxing can irritate it. The hairs are curly, and when they start to grow back in it's not unusual for a few of them to become ingrown and form painful, infected ingrown hairs. Waxing can hurt and can cause nasty burns if you don't know what you are doing, but it works for longer. Laser removal is permanent but expensive and some-what painful to undergo (the women I know who have undergone laser hair removal say it's kind of like being snapped *there* by a rubber band each time the laser fires). Life is about choices. As one of my fashion conscious 8th grade girls ruefully observed about some painful but stylish shoes she wore, "beauty hurts, Mr. Beck."(15)

Question: How do you prevent getting a saggy vagina?
How can a vagina be loose?

Answer: Well, not being sure what a "saggy vagina" is, let me lay out some possibilities. The lips of the vulva and the tissue around it can vary infinitely, like everything else about humans.

You are pretty much born with what you have, and if it looks "saggy" to you, sorry. There are, believe it or not, plastic surgeries for tweaking these things too. These can be painful, and it's hard not to ask why one would do that. But, appearance, even "down there" is really important to some people.

It seems more likely that this person if referring to a "prolapsed uterus/vagina," where the muscles, tendons, and supporting tissue holding the uterus and vagina in place are damaged during a difficult pregnancy or delivery, and the uterus actually sags down and pushes the vaginal canal tissue out the vaginal opening. This can be corrected surgically, and it has become somewhat less common in modern, healthy women and girls who maintain good fitness and practice the "kegel exercises."

Kegel exercises are performed by tensing and relaxing the muscles of the "pelvic floor" that support the uterus, vagina, intestines, and other lower abdominal organs. How? Squeeze the muscles that you use to stop peeing. These are also the muscles that contract the vagina, anus, and so on. To get used to the idea, next time you pee, girls, try repeatedly stopping and starting the flow of urine. That's exercising your kegel muscles. It can be done anywhere, anytime, not just when you are peeing. Most doctors recommend that you do this anyway to keep that area in shape and prevent "loose vaginas" and the bladder control and urine leaks that can surprise some girls and women. Kegel exercises are good for guys too both in terms of making it easier to hold off urinating in those times you need to, and in having at least some control of your ejaculation.

> **Question:** Does sperm regrow after it has distributed from the penis?
> Can one produce sperm with one testi?

Answer: Both testis continually produce MILLIONS of sperm cells *a day* for pretty much your entire life after puberty, literally until the day you die. Unlike women, men never stop making reproductive cells. It doesn't matter how much you ejaculate; you've got more sperm coming down the pipe. So, losing a testis is not that big a deal. Lance Armstrong, the now infamous bicycle racer, lost one of his testes to testicular cancer, and he has fathered a couple children with the one he has left. That's why you have two, so you have a spare.

Question: Is it bad if one of your balls hangs lower then the other?

Answer: No, it's normal, and all guys are built that way. Why? They are positioned that way so that one slides over and the other under its partner so that they don't mash each other swaying back and forth or being squeezed between your thighs like they would if they were truly side by side. Just another little evolutionary adaptation. The guys with side by side balls mashed them, injured them, and didn't father as many children as the "deformed" guys with over-under balls. So, the over-under ball genes got passed on to you, and the side by side balls guys became extinct.

Question: Is it natural for your erect penis to hurt all day and make you have trouble concentrating?

Answer: For many guys, especially in your teens, it can seem that you *always* have an erection. Yes, it can be at least somewhat painful and distracting. Girls, yes, you have periods and all that to deal with, but a penis can be a real distracting, bothersome nuisance in *every day* of our lives. Not that we want to be rid of it, or would trade it for periods and cycling hormones, but we don't get off with a free ride either. Part of growing up is dealing with that rigid tent pole and badly functioning "second brain" between our legs. That's why a lot of young guys masturbate a lot, just to remove the distraction and get some relief, at least for a while.

Question: Can you have sex if your penis isn't circumcised?

Answer: Of course you can. Billions of men around the world are *not* circumcised, and nobody was until a few thousand years ago. First, if you are not circumcised, you may not know what it is. Circumcision began as religious rite in the Jewish faith and later among Muslims as well. Male babies in both Jewish and Muslim faiths traditionally have the foreskin cut off the penis in the first few days after birth. This is done as a sign of their people's bond with God or Allah. The foreskin is the flap of skin that folds around and over the end of the penis, often described as the "turtleneck" of the penis. When erect, the penis stretches out of this flap to its full length, exposing the head of the penis. A circumcision removes the outer part of this foreskin. Circumcised penises lack this "turtleneck" so that the head of the penis is exposed, erect or not.

There has been a lot of controversy about circumcision in recent years, with some people arguing passionately that it is cruel and unnecessary mutilation of babies. The other side argues with equal force that it improves hygiene and cleanliness. There are valid studies that indicate that men with circumcised penises are less likely to pick up STDs and infections in their penis, with the counterargument being that simple cleanliness and proper personal hygiene (dude, wash your penis!) can easily overcome this. It is common practice in American hospitals to circumcise male babies for the hygienic reasons mentioned above, though nowadays parents are presented with the pros and cons of both options and allowed to make the decision. (8)

Question: If you cut your penis in half will it still work?

Answer: Well, are we talking about splitting it down the middle or cutting off the outer half? Does either of these options sound like a good thing? Would you like to have this done to your penis, or the penis of someone you love?

While modern surgical techniques can repair a lot of damage, I don't think any doctor would claim that your penis will work as well after cutting it in half as it did before. Depending on the actual damage done and how good the surgery is, you might retain some function, but it's just not going to be the same...

Question: How come it takes longer to get an erection while in a colder environment?

Answer: Nature has evolved mechanisms to protect our bodies and make sure we don't lose body heat. The penis may be important for species survival, but it needs a lot of warm blood flowing to it to get an erection. If the body senses severe cold, it reflexively restricts blood flow to the extremities (hands, feed, and so on), including the penis, so that the body's warmth is saved for the important internal organs, making it harder for you to get an erection until the body, or at least the penis, feels warm and safe. The penis may be very special to you, but the body protects the individual's internal organs and survival first.

Question: What is blue balls?

Answer: When a male human is sexually aroused, blood engorges (fills) not only the penis, but the testes and surrounding tissue as well. When the man has an ejaculation/orgasm, the constricted blood vessels that cause that engorgement relax and let the blood flow normally back to the rest of the body. That's why you lose your erection quickly after ejaculation. When a man has been aroused for a long time without the release of ejaculation/orgasm, this backed- up blood can cause pressure in the testes that can cause them to ache like they were bruised a bit, hence the term "blue balls." It goes away by itself over a time period that varies between minutes to a couple hours and causes no physical harm. Girls: yes, it is a real condition, but it does not oblige you to provide any kind of sex to relieve it. Guys are very good at doing that themselves if needed.

Question: What is blowing a load?

Answer: One of the nearly infinite number of slang terms for ejaculation.

Question: How does your penis know when to give spurm to the vagina?

Answer: The penis "knows" when the nerves in the skin of the penis have been stimulated enough during intercourse or masturbation that they trigger the reflexive contractions of the muscles of the prostate gland and cause ejaculation.

Questions: What is a G-spot?
Why do girls have a squishy thing in their vagina? What is it? Why do they need it?

Answer: The "G-spot" was named after a German gynecologist named Ernst Grafenberg who first suggested its existence in a scientific paper in 1950. It became a popular topic of sexuality discussions, self-help books, and research after the publication of the book *The G Spot and Other Recent Discoveries in Human Sexuality* by Ladas and other authors in 1982. Its actual existence is still a matter of some scientific argument, but generally it's agreed that many – but by no means all – women are aware of a pressure-sensitive area from one to three inches inside on the front wall of the vagina. Physically, it can be felt as a patch of sort of wrinkly ("squishy") tissue in that location. Pressure stimulation on this area manually or by the penis during sexual intercourse can lead to intense orgasms and is often connected to female ejaculation or "squirting." It is another one of those "either you do or you don't" issues. Women who experience it swear by it, while others don't know what all the fuss is about because it doesn't work for them. Keep in mind that the clitoris is still the center of arousal for all women, while the G spot is often much harder to pin down, if you can find it at all. Women can have very intense, satisfying sexual experiences whether the G spot works for them or not. Again, as I keep saying, normal is what's normal for you.

Question: How do birds have sex? Or any type of animal?

Answer: All mammals have "penis in vagina" sex, with organs that are pretty much the same as humans. There are variations, but not big ones. Whales, for example, have completely retractable penises, and the testes are inside the body both for streamlining and to keep the sperm the right temperature.

Reptiles have twinned sex organs, with side by side penises in the males and side by side ovaries and uterus organs for forming eggs. Older more primitive groups of birds like ducks and geese have a single penis and ovary, while modern, more "derived" birds have evolved without penises, have a single ovary in the female, and mate by pressing their cloaca openings (the single external opening birds and reptiles have for defecation, intercourse, and birth) together. The penises are internal in reptiles and the birds that still have them, and only come outside the body through the cloaca when erect for intercourse. So reptiles and birds have intercourse. While most fish and amphibians simply release eggs and sperm into the water for fertilization, sharks (from an evolutionary standpoint, more primitive than most fish) have the same twin penis and ovary system as reptiles. (13)

Question: Why do girls PMS?

Answer: PMS stands for Pre-Menstrual Syndrome. It refers to a number of symptoms that virtually all women experience in some form in the days just before and at the beginning of the menstrual period. These can include any, all or virtually none of the following in varying degrees of severity:

- *Irritability, moodiness, emotional sensitivity, or mild depression (these issues of mood are what most guys think of when it comes to PMS, since it the part that affects them)*
- *Bloating as the body retains water*
- *Uterine cramps*
- *Food cravings*
- *Changes in bowel movements*

These symptoms are usually a variable nuisance in mature women, but they can really mess with all women and girls at some times. They can be worse some months than others, especially for young girls. In severe cases they can incapacitate a woman and be very disruptive to her life and the life of people close to her for that part of her monthly cycle. This doesn't mean that their lives or relationships stop while experiencing PMS. All women learn to deal with it to whatever extent it affects them, and even if they are experiencing it, they don't let it interfere with their lives, except in extreme cases.

As to why, it really is hormones. Guys are used to a constant hormone level, and, while it does in fact vary some, most guys are not aware of any change in their mood or body feelings day to day or month to month, other than how their experiences in life affect them.

Not so with women. Everything about their body and its hormones are changing daily throughout their reproductive life. For part of the month their hormones are telling the uterus to build up its layer of blood vessels to make ready for ovulation and possible pregnancy. Then the hormones make her produce an egg from one of the ovaries, and this is usually accompanied by a heightened interest in sex whether she is aware of it or not, because her body wants her to get pregnant while she has a fertile egg available. If she doesn't get pregnant, her hormones shift and tell her body to get rid of that uterine lining, with emotional variability as a side effect, followed by hormone-directed, often painful or at least bothersome cramps in the uterus. This is accompanied by hormone directed cravings for food to replace the blood and tissue she will lose soon. On top of that, she then has to bleed down there for a few days. Then it starts over.

Gentlemen, imagine that happening to your body every month, followed by bleeding for a few days out of your penis, which would require paraphernalia like absorbent inserts for you jock strap or boxer briefs. You might get cranky too, at least some of the time.

Question: If a person has no testis, can there be metal testis inserted into the scrotum?

Answer: Men who have had testicular cancer or injuries requiring one or both testes to be removed can have artificial plastic ones inserted into the scrotum to maintain normal appearance and feel. I don't know about metal ones. The additional weight would probably eventually stretch and cause problems for the scrotum. It's a lot of trouble just to be able to say you have "brass ones."

MASTURBATION

Question: Is it possible to have sex with yourself?

Answer: Yes, that's what we call "masturbation." It means stimulating your own sex organs yourself, usually with the hands, to the point of ejaculation in boys and men and to orgasm in girls and women.

Question: Is jacking off bad for your penis?

Answer: In and of itself, no. Masturbation is pretty normal, as we discuss further below. If you are doing it constantly and you penis is getting raw and sore, that should tell you to back off a while.

Question: What is a queef, (see above) and how much can guys giz at once and how many times a day?
If you masterbate too many times can you loose all of your spurm?
Do you ever run out of sperm if you masturbate too much?

Answer: *(Note: we always start any discussion of masturbation with the advice that attitudes toward masturbation vary a lot between families and depending on religious beliefs. Students are advised to keep these attitudes in mind.)* The average ejaculation is about a teaspoon (a cubic centimeter or two). As they start masturbating young men and boys can do it a lot, in some cases several times a day at least. However, the volume of ejaculated semen produced will go down with repetition, as will the amount of sperm in the ejaculate. Now, don't go thinking, "Cool, if I masturbate a lot, I won't get a girl pregnant!" Not so. We are talking reducing the number of sperm cells from tens of millions per ejaculation to just millions, and ***it only takes one sperm to do the job.***

The other thing to keep in mind is that, like anything else, you can do too much of a good thing. If the penis (or the clitoris and vulva for that matter) gets sore or raw, you might want to back off for a few days.

> **Question:** Is masturbating addicting?
> Why is masturbating so addictive.
> Is it bad to masterbate every day? Or twice a day?
> Is it bad to masterbate more than 4 times a day?
> Is it bad to masterbate like 7 or 8 times a day?
> How often should people masturbate (at last, proper spelling!!!)?

Answer: Keep in mind the reminder that some families and various religions can have strong views on masturbation and its acceptability. Scientifically, it's perfectly normal and even healthy for young people and adults to masturbate, sometimes quite a lot (a number of times a day). Like any activity that activates the pleasure centers and chemicals of the brain, it's possible to become addicted to sex and masturbation. However, addiction to masturbation is pretty rare. As I mentioned, if your sex organs are getting sore, you should stop for a while *(duh!!)*, and if you keep masturbating anyway despite the soreness, you may have a problem. Similarly, if your masturbation is getting in the way of things you need to do, like a social life, homework, and family relations, you may have a problem.

So, common sense should prevail (not always easy in the realm of sex and young people), and you should talk to someone if you really think you have a problem. These people can include parents (they were young and did it too). Pastors, rabbis, and priests are all trained counselors in these areas nowadays, as well as the teachers and counselors here at school too. I know it sounds horribly embarrassing, but it's just not a big deal to these trained, understanding people. But truly, normally, this type of addiction is pretty rare for people your age, though not unheard of.

Question: Are you suppost to masterbate?
When is the proper age to start masterbating?
What's the average age for a kid to masterbate? Is it normal to masterbate? When did you start to jack off? (Fat chance I'll answer that one, aside from the ground rule that the kids don't get to ask me about my sex life any more than I get to ask about theirs.)
What is the proper way to masturbate?

Answer: There's no "proper" or "normal" age. Babies and toddlers often discover that it feels good to poke and rub around down there as soon as they learn to use their hands and bodies. More than one flustered parent has had to teach the child that just learned to walk not to do "that" anywhere they get the notion, and that their bedroom or bathroom is the proper location if they must. Your body tells you when and if you are interested. Most commonly it starts along with puberty as your body begins to sexually mature and you begin to understand and explore sexual feelings.

Again, from a medical/scientific standpoint, there's nothing more normal than masturbation for boy/men or girls/women. Let's face it: masturbation is almost always the first sex you have. Importantly, it is how we learn much about what we do and don't like in sex. There are studies that show that people get as much or more pure sexual satisfaction from masturbation as they do from sex with a partner, though obviously sex with a partner you love is a whole different thing. If, however, you or your family have strong religious or moral beliefs about masturbation, you may find the guilt and/or emotional discomfort tough to bear, and you need to keep these considerations in mind. Like all issues regarding sex, it's a very private decision.

Further, there is nothing wrong with you if you have little or no interest in masturbating at your age. The mantra of this book, if nothing else, is that we all vary infinitely, and normal is what is normal for you, as long as you are not damaging yourself or others.

As to the proper way, always say please and thank you, and wash your hands afterwards. The rest you'll have to figure out on your own...

Question: How come when you jack your penis off (as opposed to what other part of the body, I'd like to know) you feel like you want to pass out?

Answer: When you have an erection and an orgasm, it can cause a drop in blood pressure that can make you temporarily dizzy. It passes quickly. This is also why people often have sex lying down.

Question: Sometimes I get horny but I don't want to watch porn cause my Mom will get mad. What should I do?

Answer: Good for mom. She should upgrade the family's web access software so she doesn't have to worry about it. Dude, this is why masturbation was invented, to take care of being horny without the need for porn. You don't need porn to masturbate, and while I have no problem with porn for adults, what young guys see in online porn nowadays can give you a really distorted image of sex and what it's about for most people. I know it may be almost inconceivable to someone your age, but billions of young men through history and all the way down to the very present have dealt with being horny by masturbating, *completely without access to porn -- on line or anywhere else !!!*

Question: How do you feel about masturbation? Should it be done instead of sex? Should people our age be doing it?

Answer: My "feelings" about masturbation are not terribly important. As I've noted elsewhere, all the scientific evidence indicates that masturbation is totally normal. If you are going to masturbate, the only important "should" is to do it at an appropriate time and place, in private. However, there are people who on moral or religious grounds don't think you should masturbate, and you have to look at your personal and family attitudes toward the issue.

One of the most important, and oldest, uses of masturbation is as a substitute for sexual intercourse with someone else. People have *always* used masturbation to relieve sexual tension when they are not in a relationship or when they are in circumstances where they cannot have sex. That's one of the best uses of masturbation, and it has certainly kept any number of people out of trouble over the centuries by making it possible to relieve that sexual "pressure" without the complications of a sexual relationship or hook-ups with people you don't know. These benefits apply equally to males and females.

> **Question:** I haven't ejaculated yet but I think I've made pre-ejaculate. Why am I getting pre-ejaculate buy no sperm when I masturbate?

Answer: It may be simply that your body hasn't started producing actual semen yet. Almost certainly it will in the next couple of years. Just to be sure we are talking about the same thing, pre-ejaculate are the few drops of clear, slippery fluid that come out of the penis before actual ejaculation. Ejaculate itself can vary a lot, but it is usually:

- *Thicker, and some sort of milky colored compared to the clear pre-ejaculate*
- *Usually there are several squirts totaling a teaspoon or so in volume that emerge with actual ejaculation.*

If you are not having the latter happen to you in a couple years, you might want to see a doctor about it. If nothing else is going on, that is, no pain, no puss-like discharge, *and* if you are getting the sexual release and satisfaction of masturbation, I wouldn't worry for now. HOWEVER, I am NOT a doctor, so I am not qualified to diagnose these things. If you have concerns you should talk to your parents (I know, fat chance, but I hope you feel you could) and/or see a doctor.

Question: Sometimes I can't stop ejaculating it just keeps coming out.

Answer: This isn't actually a question, but a statement, perhaps even bragging? Look, eventually it stops right? You are not ejaculating now as you write or listen to my answer. So, obviously it stops at some point. If you produce a lot of semen, then that's what your body does. If you have long orgasms, then that's what you do. Enjoy it.

Questions: Should a girl finger herself, or let a guy "help her?"
Does it feel better when one masterbates, or, when a girl or guy does it for us?
How do girls masturbate?

Answer: *(Note: This is one of those questions that skirts close to the "how do I do it?" issue that we strictly avoid, versus the intent for the class to be about, "what it is." The question is a legitimate and earnest inquiry about what a girl can do, and what she should allow to be done to her.)*
Guys will always be glad to "help" you with these things. The question, of course, is, are they helping you or having fun for themselves. Keep in mind that if someone is "helping you," it's not masturbation, it's sex: a hand job. Guys, and the girls involved, may not know in their own mind – it's hard to tell sometimes. Most girls find that (at least at first) they find out much more on

their own without the "help" of someone who may have much more on their mind than helpful assistance.

As to how, remember this is not a "how to do it" class. However, since we explain that guys rub their penis with their hands when they masturbate (among other things), it is hardly inappropriate to point out that girls rub their clitoris with their hands (among other things), which as noted above is the equivalent to the penis in girls.

Masturbation for girls: a discussion for the reader: As noted above, the whole issue of masturbation for girls is, despite the apparent over-sexualization of our culture, a very cloudy issue for many, if not most, 13-14 year olds in my experience. Let's face it: guys can't avoid their penis. It's out there in plain sight from birth, and shortly thereafter they begin manipulating it for urination, fun (you know, writing your name in the snow, shooting down flies in a urinal, and so on...) and masturbation. For girls, the clitoris, that little, sensitive knob above the urethra, is fairly easy to miss, especially since we culturally avoid pointing it out at all costs. We fear over-sexualization, but we fear solid, sensible information even more. I have lovely color overhead transparencies of the female sexual anatomy approved for use in Family Life Education that show and label everything *but* the clitoris! Now, to be fair, I have other transparencies that do in fact point it out.

When I point out that not only do boys and men masturbate, but that girls and women do so as well, it's very common for students of both sexes to look at each other and me in amazement and ask, "they do??" and "how?" While I generally agree with the prohibition on explaining "how to do it" questions for this age group, this is one area where a couple sentences would clear up a lot of confusion and misinformation. So, I just say, when the subject comes up, "Girls rub their clitorises just like guys rub their penises, and for the same reasons. They can be just as imaginative as guys in coming up with ways to enjoy themselves."

If you are an Oprah fan (and even if you are not), you may have caught an episode on middle school sexuality in the spring of 2009. I highly recommend parents go to the Oprah website and use the search feature on the site to locate the "Dr. Laura Berman Sex Talk" episodes. The page has both video and audio discussions of the issue, including how to approach the sex talk with your children, and most particularly a couple different sequences on discussing sexuality with daughters, including the issue of masturbation for girls specifically as an alternative to actual sex and the issues that attend intercourse at this age. You may or may not agree with what's said, but parents should give it a serious, thoughtful listen. (14)

Question: If you jack off too much and use too much jizz, can you still have babies? If you jizz in your face, can you get zits?

Answer: Having a lot of ejaculations whether through masturbation or intercourse does reduce you sperm count. It can drop from tens of millions per ejaculation to just millions, or maybe hundreds of thousands. ***It still takes just one to cause a pregnancy! An epic amount of masturbation is not birth control!***

Acne is cause by hormones and skin oil. Getting ejaculate on your face will not help or hurt your acne, but it may indicate bad technique, and if you leave it there, people will know what you have been doing...

Question: Does masterbation cause pubic acne? Can you get acne from masterbating too much with unclean hands?

Answer: Masturbation itself has no connection with pubic acne or any other kind of acne. Acne is acne, caused by hormonal shifts, excess oil in the skin, or shaving in that area, all of which can be made worse by less-than-stellar hygiene. So in that sense, masturbating with dirty hands can't help, but it's not the cause of acne down there or anywhere else.

Question: Can you have sex with a hotdog?
(Another question from a girl.)
If you have sex with a hot dog, can it break off in there?

Answer: Well, first you should buy the hot dog dinner and a couple drinks, and then maybe after the third date...

Physically, there is nothing to prevent it. The typical hot dog is smaller in diameter (that is, narrower) than a typical penis while being about the same length. HOWEVER, it is not sterile, and you will introduce bacteria into the vagina that can cause an infection. I realize that penises are not sterile either, but the point is the bacteria on a healthy penis are ones a vagina normally encounters and are not the same as those on any hotdog. So, obviously most doctors would not recommend inserting hot dogs or other household objects in vaginas, even if you manage to do so without problems. So, yes, if you use a hot dog, it could break and you would have to get it out. Again, the vagina is not bottomless, and most girls should be able to reach up and get the broken piece. If not, you may need to go to the doctor so he/she can. But, do you want to have to explain how that happened?..

Question: Do chicks masterbate as much as guys?

Answer: Historically, on average, no. Like everything else about humans, there is a huge range of "normal." Certainly it is just as "normal" for girls to masturbate as it is for boys, and there are any number of girls/women who masturbate as much as boys/men. It's also perfectly normal, especially at this point in your life, for a girl to feel like "OMG! Give me a break, what's all the fuss about, and leave me alone!" There's nothing wrong with you if you don't feel like your favorite bad girl on *Gossip Girl* or *90210*. Many girls go through an exploratory phase when they masturbate quite a lot, then taper off as they get into relationships and/or learn what they like. There is some thought that girls/women don't masturbate as much because culturally they have been taught from a young age that it is dirty and improper for girls and that masturbation is something only "sexually insatiable" boys do. As our culture has moved away from this view, it appears that more girls are feeling more comfortable about masturbation and that the differences are being reduced. Almost all studies of the sex drive and desire of the two sexes show that men want sex more frequently and consistently than girls. There are some recent studies that indicate that women's sex drives match that of men overall when studied *independently of cultural factors*. Even if this is true, girls and women's sexuality tends to be more cyclical than guys', and even if they feel the need to masturbate a lot some of the time, they may find that they are simply not that way all the time the way guys often seem to be. Guys are sexually "on" pretty continuously. On average, sexual desire in girls/women tends to peak a couple weeks after their period starts when they ovulate, then begins to taper off for the rest of the month before rising again as their menstrual cycle moves through the month. So it would be normal for many girls to masturbate more at some times of the month than others, though again "normal" is a tricky thing, and no one should worry if they are not particularly interested most of the time, or are doing it all the time. **Normal is what is normal for you.** (14, 21)

Question: Why do girls squirt when they masturbate?

Is female ejaculation real?

Answer: Squirting, or properly, "female ejaculation," is another one of those "either you do or you don't" happenings. A female ejaculation happens at orgasm to some women some of the time when the girl or woman has the vaginal and uterine contractions that go with orgasm. There is still a lot of research and some debate on the subject, but most scientists who study these things now agree that the female ejaculation is *not* just losing control and peeing during orgasm, as many women who have experienced it fear. The fluid is not urine but a complex, clear fluid that has been described as having a smell something like hay or cut grass. It is produced in some little \-understood glands that surround and feed into the urethra in front of the vagina. These are called "Skene's glands" and are the equivalent in women to the prostate gland in men. Like I say, nature adapts the same hardware in each sex for that sex's purposes.

Female ejaculation is associated with intense orgasms, but many if not most women can and do have intense orgasms without fluid and ejaculation. Like I keep saying, there is no point in worrying about what is normal. Some women do this during masturbation or sex with a partner; some don't. Some do it most of the time; some only rarely if at all. The porn industry has made this a big deal, but it has no bearing on how sexual someone is, or on how much they enjoy sex. Some people find it a real nuisance; others think is a sure sign that the sex was great. Don't worry about it either way. (21, 22)

Question: How come when you jack off most of the time it drips. How come it doesn't shoot up in the air?

One time when I ejaculated, I measured it and it went 4 feet . Is that Normal? Why is it when I masterbate my sperm shoots out & lands on my feet? Serious question!

Answer: Again, people vary. How far it shoots and the thickness and gooeyness of semen depends on how much liquid you have been drinking, how often you have ejaculated, and on normal variations in your body chemistry and the muscles that contract and squirt out the semen. It may drip one time and go halfway across the room another. Some men have more powerful muscles and shoot it farther, and some don't. Remember, all nature and evolution care about is that the semen gets deposited up near the cervix at the top of the vagina. The swimming sperm do the rest, so it doesn't really matter how far it shoots. As long as it comes out at all, feels good and there's no pain or indication of an infection, don't worry about it.

I would like to know how the four foot ejaculation was measured. Most men don't have the time or the hands to hold a ruler when that happens... As to the semen on the feet issue: we are in 8th grade physical science. We have studied gravity. You know what direction gravity will pull something shot into the air. If you are standing up, where would the semen land *other* than on or near your feet?

Question: Is it normal if I can suck my own dick? If you take out some ribs can you give yourself a blow job?

Answer: Nope, that would not be considered normal, because most boys and men just do not have the flexibility to do so. Many have tried, and a very few can actually pull it off. The few are often the envy of their friends.

Removing ribs to make this possible is an urban legend attributed to various kinky celebrities over the years. I can't confirm if it has ever actually happened.

Question: Do girls jack off with tampons?
Can you lose your virginity to a tampon?
Do the tampon and penis go in the same hole?
Do girls get orgasms when they put in a tampon?

Answer: All right, girls, a show of hands. How many of you are turned on by using tampons? Especially during that time of the month? What, no one? Now, I'm not going to say this has never crossed a girl's mind—their minds can come up with just as much sexual weirdness as a guy's. But, as any girl will tell you (then again, maybe they'd just punch you for being rude if you asked), tampons are not the easiest or most comfortable things to use, at least while you are learning how. They have very little in common with a penis or anything sexually interesting, other than that they go in the vagina. Furthermore, masturbation for women has *much* more to do with the clitoris than it does with putting small random objects in the vagina. It's always a shock for guys to realize that.

In a real sense, there is no connection between tampon use and virginity, though there are some religions and cultures that teach otherwise. Tampons are smaller in diameter and length compared to a penis, and most women who have never had sexual intercourse can learn to use them without problems.

Question: Is it true that when you jack-off your arm can get bigger than the other?

Answer: I don't have any scientific data on this. It seems at least somewhat logical that if you did a lot of masturbating and *only* used one arm to do so, you might see some difference. Keep in mind that masturbating does not put a lot of strain on your muscles, so it isn't going to build a lot of new muscle bulk. If you are actually worried about this, you could alternate arms, our use both arms. You're welcome...

Question: Can you jackoff with a condom on?

Answer: Sure you can. It may take you a little longer to get there, but it's much tidier—none of that semen on the shoes stuff.

Question: Someone told me if you masterbate you will go blind and grow hair on your hands?
If you masterbate to much can you go blind?

Answer: So, how many blind, hairy-handed teenagers have you met lately? You realize that if that saying were true, the entire male half of the species would be blind and have to shave their hands. And that's hard to do when you are blind. The same observation would probably go for most of the women too. This *ancient* warning about masturbation has been around for decades, if not centuries. Embarrassed gym teachers were explaining that this was not true in health classes when I was in junior high. It goes back to a time when many, if not most, people thought masturbation was unhealthy and evil, and the myth was created to keep boys from doing so.

Question: I have a urge to put my hand on my cock. What is wrong with me.

Why does my penis always want me to jack him off?

Answer: Nothing that isn't "wrong" with most teenage boys and most men, which is to say, nothing at all. You feel the need to masturbate. It's normal and not wrong, unless you can't control the urge and start touching yourself at inappropriate times—then it's just creepy.

CONCEPTION, CONTRACEPTION, AND BIRTH

Question: I haven't had my period in 4 months, am I pregnant?
I think I'm pregnant, what should I do?

Answer: The immediate question is, "Did you have unprotected sex during or before that four month time frame?" If you had unprotected sex (or even if you had "protected" sex: remember, birth control can fail), then you could be pregnant. If you have not had sex, protected or otherwise, you are not pregnant. So, if you have had sex, protected or otherwise, get a home pregnancy test to make a quick check and then see a doctor. If you have the slightest thought that you are pregnant, especially four months pregnant, you should see a doctor to get proper pre-natal (pre-birth) care for yourself and the baby you are carrying. By four months along, you should be having other pregnancy symptoms, like some weight gain, enlarged breasts, possibly nausea/morning sickness, and so on.

On the other hand, you could just be a 13-14 year old girl whose menstrual cycle has not settled down yet, whether you have had sex or not. It's very common to go months without a period early on, and it's just as common to have some kind of period in less than the normal 28-29 days, until your body regulates itself into a normal cycle. *However, don't buy into wishful thinking.* **If you think you may be pregnant, you need to get a pregnancy test AND see a doctor as soon as possible.** *Don't lie to yourself, don't delay, don't hope it will go away if you ignore it, don't do all the stupid things that people think kids your age do. Whoever you are, please see me privately soon. If you are uncomfortable talking to me about it, please talk to our school counselor, your parents or a doctor.*

Note to reader: Every couple years I get questions like this. My experience is that the girl has never to my knowledge been pregnant for the reasons described above. One upsetting thing that has happened to me is that the question slips with these two questions were put in my TMI question box after the last day I was able to take questions, and I did not discover them until I was sorting through the slips a month after the school year ended for the purposes of writing this book. Until that point, I thought I had answered all the submitted question slips for that year. I have no idea who the girl was, and there was no way to follow up and find out which of my 200 8th graders submitted the slips.

Question: If the girl takes a birth control pill before having unprotected sex, can they still get pregnant?

Answer: *YES, YES, YES!!* The various birth control pills (and there are dozens, if not hundreds, of brands today) all rely on you taking them consistently, ***every day***, preferably at the same time of day, in order to be effective. ***One pill by itself does virtually nothing to protect from pregnancy***. Birth control pills usually come in a package of all the pills for a monthly menstrual cycle, one for each day of the month, or for however many days that brand has you take them. If you start taking the pill in the middle of your cycle, you will still need to take it a full month before having unprotected sex, because you have probably already ovulated and are ripe for getting pregnant. If you start taking it during your period, you probably will be protected to some extent by the time your period is over, but virtually all doctors will still insist that you take the pill a full cycle (from the beginning of one menstrual period though the end of the next period you have) before having unprotected sex. Again, you have to take the pill at the same time every day. If you forget a day or two, it can fail and you can get pregnant, whether you take the rest of the month's pills or not. Think how often you "forget" to do your chores, your homework, to call a friend you promised to call. You cannot forget the pill, and you have to *exactly follow* your doctor's instructions for the brand of pills you are taking.

This is one of those things you need to look at before having sex. Are you up to the responsibility of doing these things? It is in fact *more mature, not less* to realize that, "Hey, I'm still a kid, and I don't want to have to remember these things all the time." But then, you are not ready for sex if you can't or don't want to deal with those responsibilities.

Question: Does Mountain DewTM lower your sperm count?

Answer: No. This is another urban legend. There were some studies many years ago that showed that massive doses of the yellow dye used to color Mountain Dew™ had some effect on the sperm count of mice. But other studies found no measureable effect on regular humans consuming any possible amount of the soft drink, which does not contain massive amounts of the dye. Mountain Dew™ is NOT birth control.

Question: When you are raped can you get pregnant?

Answer: Yes, of course, unfortunately. Millions of women are raped all over the world every year in wars, by "friends," as well as by strangers. Many get pregnant. If you are ovulating, and a viable sperm gets to the egg, you can get pregnant. It doesn't matter how the sperm got there.

Question: How do cramps work? What exactly are they?

Answer: The term "cramps" usually refers to the strong contractions of the muscular uterus as it works to squeeze out and expel the blood and lining of the uterus during a woman's period. Like strong contractions of other muscles in the body, they can be painful. Typically they are stronger just before and during the first couple days of your period, then taper off. Cramps can be extremely painful, to the point of incapacitation, while other women don't even notice them. Many women find them worse while they are younger, during their first few years of having periods, and not as bad later. Some women find that an orgasm can relieve or reduce cramps; others find it makes no difference.

Question: How are babies made?
What is breast feeding?
What does breast milk taste like?

Answer: Whoa! The bottom line question. Babies are made when sperm contained in semen, deposited in the vagina during sexual intercourse (erect penis inserted into the vagina, followed by ejaculation), swim up the vagina, through the cervical opening into the uterus, then up through the uterus to the fallopian tubes (check out the overhead). Sperm swim up both fallopian tubes, but almost always only one has an egg cell floating down it, having been released by the woman's ovary that month. One – and only one—sperm unites with the egg cell or ovum and fertilizes it. This fertile egg cell begins dividing by the cellular mitosis process (7th grade science, people!) as it floats down into the uterus. Assuming all goes well, it sticks to the side of the uterus and begins growing there, eventually forming a baby fetus. The blood supply in the uterine wall joins with the baby's blood supply through the umbilical cord and the placenta to transfer nutrients and oxygen to the baby from the mother. After nine months of growth, the uterus begins birth contractions and pushes the baby out through the cervix and vagina during the birth process.

As to breast feeding, that's what breasts are really for, not just a place to put implants. Breasts themselves are mostly fat tissue. Around the nipples there are groups of milk-producing glands and ducts. These evolved from sweat glands that became adapted to providing nutrients to the young of mammals. The milk produced by the breasts is, surprise, surprise, perfectly suited for nourishing human babies, who get the milk by sucking on the nipples on the breasts. Babies are born with an instinct to do this, and will feed immediately after birth.

Breast milk is thin, like skim milk, slightly yellowish in color, and quite sweet, sort of like the milk in the bottom of a cereal bowl after you've eaten all the cereal.

Note to reader: I know, by 8th grade you'd think they would know this one, especially nowadays. Yet there is still a *huge* disparity in the knowledge kids have at this point in their life. Some sat down with Mommy and Daddy at age three with all the *Where Do Babies Come From?* books and have been authoritatively explaining it all to their friends ever since. On the other hand, I had a really nice boy a couple years ago who was being raised by a grandmother (having been taken away from dysfunctional parents) who couldn't face discussing *any* of this with a growing boy. The poor kid knew nothing and asked everything, including the three questions above, plus all the really gross street language/ sex act questions that his friends prompted him to ask because he was so clueless that he would in fact ask anything. The fact is, most students are somewhere in between these extremes. Students in our district get specific sex education from 5th grade on, and most of them know these basics. However, we have a significant number that transfer in from local Catholic schools that end in 7th grade, and many of these students have not had the same sex ed experience those in our district have. The same applies to students who arrive from other parts of the country in our often transient military population students.

Question: Why do girls release blood during their
period?
What's a period?

Answer: Well, this is the second part of the question above about babies. If the girl/woman does not get pregnant, then the lining of blood vessels and blood on the inside of the uterus that would nourish a growing fetus breaks down and is shed and expelled by the uterus once a month. This is the "period." While it appears to be blood – and it mostly is – it also includes tissue and shed blood vessels from the inside of the uterus. This process can take from two to ten days, but it usually averages something around a week or less. Its timing can be very irregular when the girl is younger, happening every couple weeks, or going months in between as noted above, but with time it settles down in most women to a pretty predictable 28-29 day cycle.

Question: If a woman is pregnant and she's having sex, can the guy feel the baby? Can you break the water bag?

Answer: No, in any normal pregnancy, the pregnancy has no effect on sex, and the man certainly cannot feel the baby. Further, there is virtually no danger of breaking the amniotic sac (the "water bag") that the baby floats in during the pregnancy. Most doctors nowadays will allow and even encourage sex during a normal healthy pregnancy up to and even into the ninth month of pregnancy. *Again, this is during a normal, healthy pregnancy, and each pregnancy is different, even for women who have had one or two already.* If it is a high-risk pregnancy, where the woman is known to have a risk of miscarriage or other health issues affected by sexual activity, then sex would be discouraged during the pregnancy. You should ALWAYS be under a doctor's care during any pregnancy so you can discuss this and any other issue connected with your pregnancy.

Question: Is there anything worse than labor?

Answer: Well, define worse. Certainly most doctors will tell you that men could not handle it in any way. Women who have had the experience liken it to having a bowel movement with a watermelon. But the fact is that there are six billion of us on this planet, and some woman gave birth to all of them. Many women gladly go through the process repeatedly because the fact is: you survive it, and our memories are very selective about not remembering the pain. If the woman is in a good relationship and wants to be a mom, she will tell you that the experience was more than worth it. Again, for some women, it's relatively easy and almost fun, for others it's a near death experience, and for most it's somewhere in between.

Question: Would a plastic bag work instead of a condom?

Answer: If you've thought of it, someone else has and tried it. Short answer: **NO!**

A plastic bag is a **very poor** substitute for a condom. First off, it doesn't seal around the top of the penis like a condom does, and that open leakiness is **not** what you want in your birth control method. It kind of defeats the whole purpose if the open top of the bag lets semen slop over onto the vagina. The bag also has corners and folds that can be pointy and uncomfortable for both partners. Not a good idea, and again, remember my lecture and Power Point. ***If you are not ready or able to take responsibility for proper birth control and safer sex practices (like getting real, quality condoms), then you need to look seriously at the fact that you are not ready for sex.***

Question: If a girl is on her period and she gets sexually active and the guy doesn't use protection, what are the chances of her being pregnant?
If you have sex with a girl thats on her period, will you get the blood on your penis and everywere on the bed?

Answer: *If* the girl is having normal, regular monthly periods, intercourse during the period, while being messy (and yes, especially during the first couple days of heavier blood flow during a girl's period, it can be quite messy), has a relatively low chance of causing pregnancy. *Not impossible, but low.* The problem is that at your age, *many* girls are NOT having regular, monthly periods, and then the chances are harder to predict. They may be ovulating at the same time they are having their period, or they may ovulate immediately after their period rather than a week or so later, so the timing that may prevent pregnancy when having sex during a normal period may be tricky if you are not having regular 28 day cycles every month. Sperm can live for three to seven days inside a woman, while the egg cells can last up to a day or two. That gives them a lot of time to hook up if you're hooking up. *The overall statistical odds of pregnancy if you are having regular, unprotected sex are about one in four each month and up to 90% over a year.* Keep that in mind.

Question: While giving birth can you accedently pull the babies head off?

Answer: If you are pulling that hard, the birth has other serious problems. Seriously, pulling the head off does not happen. Given that the plural "babies" was used, I also assume the person was talking about a multiple birth. Grammar people!

Question: If you wear 2 condoms and 1 breaks, what can happen? Are extra lubricated condoms made for less chance to have a baby?

Answer: First, the double condom myth. Wearing two condoms may make logical sense; that is, if one is good, two is better, right? Not so. A number of studies by condom manufacturers have shown that wearing two condoms at once actually increases the chance that both will fail because they rub against each other and break more easily. One high-quality condom, properly worn, is best.

Lubrication on condoms is a sterile surgical jelly that makes the condom easier to put on and more comfortable for both partners. Extra lubricated condoms are extra lubricated for comfort during intercourse, *not* for birth control. Lubrication also protects the condom and makes it less likely to break. Some lubricants have spermicidal compounds in them to kill sperm. These can be irritating to both partners and are not very effective. Most doctors now recommend against spermicidal lubricants. (16)

Question: I'm just wondering can anything go wrong and the man be pregnant?

Answer: No. Men do not have a uterus, do not produce eggs, and simply do not have the equipment to get pregnant or carry a baby. The "pregnant man" story in the news and on Oprah a couple years ago was not a man. This person was a "transgender" woman who was biologically female and who had undergone most of the hormone sex change therapies and surgeries to change her secondary sexual characteristics (like growing facial hair, reducing her breasts, and so on), but still retained a functioning uterus and vagina. This person was therefore able to carry a baby to term and give birth after being artificially inseminated by her partner using sperm from a sperm donor.

Question: How does the baby get out of the really small hole?
Um, how does a female vagina grow so big when the baby gets bigger and bigger?

Answer: The vagina may seem small to you at this age, and it is. However, the vagina and uterus are made of very stretchy muscle tissue that does in fact expand and stretch to pass a baby. The muscles of the uterus are also very strong, and their contractions are powerful enough during the birth process to squeeze and push the baby out of the stretchy vagina. It's not easy, but it works. Most of us came into the world through that little, stretchy hole. After the baby is born, the uterus and vagina shrink back to virtually the same size and shape they were before birth.

Question: Why did the baby look like rotten milk when I came out?

Answer: You are referring to the movie of childbirth we saw the other day. When a baby is born, it's often covered by part of the amniotic sac it floated in and by white mucus that can look like cottage cheese to some people. It's normal and is usually cleaned off by one of the nurses assisting in the birth immediately while they are checking the newborn's health.

Question: Can you get pregnant from anal sex?
Can you give birth through your butt hole?
Can you get pregnant up the butt hole?

Answer: First, I'm going to remind you of all the logical, practical, medical reasons why anal sex should avoided by people your age whose bodies are still changing and growing, and whose maturity and judgment (be honest with yourselves) and willingness to take the time and care anal sex requires is not always the best. The vagina is designed for sex. It's stretchy, relatively tough, and it lubricates itself to make sex possible and pleasurable. The anus and rectum do none of these things. They are much less stretchy, more delicate, and easily torn or damaged if not treated with care. Nor do the anus and rectum supply any lubrication for sexual intercourse. Plus, it often has poop in it, and the bacteria in poop can do several unpleasant things to careless anal sex practitioners. If you do damage the thin, delicate tissue in the anal/rectal area, it's very easy for these bacteria to cause painful and hard to treat infections in your butt (infections that are no fun to explain to your parents – no matter how good a relationship you have—or to your doctor). These infections can also take place in the penis that's been put into the anus and rectum – it's not designed to handle them either. This same delicacy makes it generally much easier to transmit sexually transmitted diseases of all kinds through **unprotected** anal sex. Unprotected sex of any kind is asking for trouble, but unprotected anal sex adds an additional element of risk.

Now, obviously, it's harder to get pregnant from anal sex. There is no connection between the anus/rectum/intestines and the uterus or vagina. So it's also impossible for the baby to come out the butt hole/anus. HOWEVER, you should have noticed by now *that the vagina and anus are really close to each other!* So, if you have unprotected (that is, without a condom) sex anally, at some point afterwards that semen is going to come back out of the anus, and if a little of it accidentally makes that short trip to the vagina, it is possible to get pregnant. This happens to people. Many people think, "Anal sex, whoopee! I don't have to use a condom!" Wrong again. For all the above medical/safer sex reasons, **and** to prevent pregnancy, condoms are just as important for anal sex. Further, if you are dumb enough to have vaginal sex *after* anal sex without seriously washing the penis and putting on a new condom, you can cause some very nasty vaginal infections. Seriously, think about it people... (17)

Question: Is intercourse the only way to get pregnant?
What is dry humping?

Answer: No. While intercourse is the obvious way that we are designed to get pregnant and the way most people get pregnant, Murphy's Law and the homing instincts of sperm cells make a surprising range of accidents possible. Sperm cells have one mission in their short, week-long life: "Find an egg, find an egg, find an egg…" If they are deposited in any way near enough or on the tissues of the vulva/vagina where they have access to the fluids in the vulva and vagina, they will swim with remarkable accuracy up the vagina, through the cervix, into the uterus, and up to the fallopian tubes looking for that egg. *Again, it only takes one sperm cell to do the job.*

A typical ejaculation contains *tens of millions* of sperm cells. However, the drops of clear seminal fluid that come out of the penis *before* ejaculation (what some people call "pre-cum") also contains tens of thousands of sperm cells. So, sticking the penis into the vagina, but withdrawing it before ejaculation can still get you pregnant.

"Dry humping" is when the penis rubs on the outside of a girl's exposed pubic area or underwear and ejaculates there without ever entering the vagina. Yes, it can still cause pregnancy if the semen soaks through the fabric of the undies and gets into the vulva/vagina. Fingering the vagina, if the fingers have also touched pre-cum or ejaculate, can also transmit viable sperm.

Now, the *chances of getting pregnant* by any of these accidental means are low, and nobody is going to honestly claim that these things are as likely to cause pregnancy as unprotected intercourse. However, an amazing number of girls have sat in tears telling their doctor, "but I can't be pregnant, we didn't even have sex!" They are correct, they didn't have penis in vagina sex. But you can still get pregnant if you are not careful, and a little bit unlucky.

Question: Can a girl get pregnant if she is on top during sex?

Answer: Of course she can! This idea is an enduring myth among young people who are first experiencing sex, and no doubt it is encouraged by our human flaw of wishful thinking (wanting something to be true because it sounds good, not because it is true) and probably *by young men trying to come up with reasons to have sex.* Once again, it only takes one sperm cell to start a pregnancy, and millions of them end up there at the top of the vagina by the cervix whether the girl is on top or not. And remember, the little guys swim vigorously. They are too small to worry about gravity. Seriously, people…

Question: Can you get a horse pregnant?

Answer: So, what grade did you get in 7th grade life science? You know, or should know, that the genes from species as different as horses and humans will not allow for a living crossbreed. Besides, no self-respecting horse would have sex with you, and they make their feelings clear with very nasty—sometimes fatal—kicks.

Question: Can a 15 yr old make love with a 25 yr old and still produce a kid

Answer: First, let me remind you that in every state in the United States, it is illegal for a 25 year old to have sex with a 15 year old, unless they are married with the younger person's parents' permission.

Now, the sex of the participants is not stated in this question, but the short answer is, absolutely. Certainly virtually all 25 year olds of either sex are fully matured physically and thus capable of being a mother or father. At 15, most girls produce viable eggs and can get pregnant. Very simply, if you have had or are having your period , you can get pregnant (and in some cases, it's possible even if the girl hasn't had a period), and most girls have started having periods by 15, though it is not unusual for at least some girls to have it start later. Most boys are producing effective sperm by that age, but not all. So again, it is absolutely possible, and it has happened, many times.

Question: Shows like "Teen Mom" and "16 and Prego" on MTV make me want to get prego.

Answer: Not really a question, but a troubling statement. I freely admit that this one baffles me as a man. I understand the instinctive desire to have a baby that is present in many women and girls. That's perfectly normal. I do not understand how a human with a functioning brain can possibly think that there is *anything* good or positive about having a baby as an unmarried (or married for that matter, given the divorce statistics of married teens) teenage mother before being psychologically, financially and mentally ready for motherhood.

Nothing, repeat, nothing about the situation is good for the mother or baby. Statistically, unless you have the resources of a wealthy family, you are pretty much guaranteeing that you and the baby will be poor and unmarried for life. Your chances of a higher education, good job, and of raising a child who will be successful in school—and therefore in life—all go *way down*. You know this if you pay the slightest attention to the news and in school.

Now, at this point, some dreamy-eyed girl always points out that she knows somebody who knows somebody that made it work. Sarah Palin's daughter Bristol is an example in many people's mind. But, she comes from a wealthy, supportive family. This idealized girl of a teenager's fantasies somehow completed college (probably with a lot of financial support and child care from her parents or friends), got a good job, and raised a great kid. There are always exceptions. There are 90 year-old, three-pack-a-day smokers, but nobody will tell you the smoking is what got them to 90. That's just not the way to bet on how the rest of your life turns out. The great, great majority of girls who are teen moms are poor, often on government welfare. So are their kids, who also have a much higher chance of doing poorly in school, of having health issues, of committing crimes and going to jail, and of having babies as teenagers themselves. Period.

Others take their cue from all the single-mom Hollywood stars. Granted, no cultural group seem worse at birth control than the current generation of Hollywood stars. Girls forget, of course, that these people make more money for a single movie or a few months of TV shows than the average person will make in a lifetime at a well-salaried job. They have nice homes, full time nannies, private schools, college trust funds, and drivers to deliver the kids where they need to be. Most important, while they may be young, they are ADULTS, not teens. You may or may not agree with their choices, but they have earned the right to make them by being adults who are not dependent on parents or the government to take care of them. They are wealthy people who have an ability to support their offspring in ways that no teenage girl and no one but members of the wealthiest families can hope to.

The fact that girls can actually think that being a mom as an unmarried teenager is a good option simply proves what adults and cultures all over the world have always known about teenagers. The part of your brain that thinks logically and looks at the long term results and consequences of your actions doesn't work right yet. It has not finished growing yet, and it is unfortunately one of the last parts of your brain to develop. This is a biological fact, and it's why parents and cultures do so many things to restrict and protect you until you are grown up enough to usually avoid really dumb ideas.

Sorry, but you know it's true. (18, 19)

SEXUALLY TRANSMITTED DISEASES AND INFECTIONS (STDS AND STIS)

Note to reader: Next to pregnancy, few topics in teenage sexuality have the combination of wishful thinking and misinformation to compare with the cloud of nonsense that surrounds STDs/STIs. Being teenagers, the assumption is that these things only happen to other people, particularly "sluts" of both the male and female kinds. Since they themselves are "nice" kids from "nice" neighborhoods who only have sex with "nice" people, these diseases can never happen to them. And, if somehow this unthinkable thing happens, there must be some pill or medicine in this modern era that will cure it in a few days—because, well, just because that's the way it should be.

Question: Is there a certain age that you can't get herbes (yes, that's how they spelled it!)or can you get herbes by holding hands?

Answer: H-e-r-*P*-e-s is a viral disease transmitted by skin to skin contact. You can catch it at any age. Most commonly, it is transmitted by oral, vaginal, or anal sex. It is **most likely** to be transmitted when one of the partners is having an outbreak of the small, painful, or itchy blisters that herpes can cause, specifically with sexual contact with these blisters. **However,** it is possible – though much less likely—to transmit it even when the person is **not having an outbreak**, again through skin to skin contact. Holding hands is a highly unlikely way to transmit the disease unless there is an outbreak blister on a hand, which is uncommon. It's virtually impossible to get it from toilet seats or sharing a drinking cup or the like.

Herpes is for life. There is no cure. Drugs like Valtrex ™ can limit and prevent outbreaks and shorten the outbreaks when they happen, but they do not cure the disease. Many medical estimates show that 50-80% of adults have either or both the genital and oral form of herpes. A cold sore **is** herpes, usually the oral kind. But you can have either oral or genital herpes in both places, mouth and genitals, and you can't tell the difference by looking at the sore. They look the same. Many people carry the disease virus their whole life without showing any symptoms (outbreaks of the blisters). These people are less likely to transmit the disease, but they very definitely can. Condoms help greatly in preventing transmission, but do not guarantee prevention. Sexual activity and kissing should be strictly avoided if the one of the partners is having an outbreak.

Question: Can you surgecly cut herpes off?

Answer: No. The herpes virus actually lives in the nerve cells near the skin, but inside the body. Only when they become active—for whatever reason—do they affect the skin and cause the blister sores. It cannot be surgically removed, and, as noted above, once you have it, you have it for life.

Question: Can you get HIV or herpes or any other
STD by sucking dick?
--- and ---
Can you get a STD from eating a girls
vagina

Answer: Yes, of course. Virtually all STDs can be transmitted by oral sex, whether you're putting your mouth on a penis or on a vulva/vagina. Germs like warm, wet places. Your mouth and throat will do just fine for STD germs.

HIV is relatively difficult to transmit orally compared to some STDs, but that should hardly be reassuring: both HIV and herpes are permanent STDs with no cures in sight. Just to pile it on, a lot of recent studies show a rapid increase in oral and throat warts and cancers caused by the Human Papillomavirus (HPV) in *both men and women*. HPV is another STD that is permanent once you have it. There is no cure. This disease, which can cause genital warts and cervical cancer, is increasingly causing warts and cancers in the mouth and throat. This can only be due to a lot of unprotected oral sex. Fun. This is why doctors now recommend that both girls *and* boys get the Gardicil™ vaccine for HPV as early as age 10.

Question: Someone said that a girl giving a guy
oral sex is good for the girls mouth/
teeth because the cum/ejaculation is
good and kills germs in the mouth. Is
that true?
-- and --
If you give a BJ is the person clean?

Answer: Ahh... The lies and creative wishful thinking boys will invent to get a girl to go down on them. No it is NOT true.

Now, the ejaculate from someone who does not have an STD is pretty harmless stuff. It's actually high in protein and so on. But, it has NO special properties as far as keeping anyone's mouth healthy. Since it has protein and calories, it can contribute to tooth decay like any other "food" you eat or drink.

However, if a guy ejaculates in your mouth you have to realize that you have just had unprotected sex with that person. This means you have decided that: 1) you know he hasn't had sex with anyone else to be exposed to STDs, or 2) he's protected himself if he *has* had sex with someone else, plus 3) he's been tested for STDs, so he knows the truth, but 4) that it's okay that he may or may not know the truth himself; he doesn't have to be lying to be wrong, and finally 5) he wouldn't lie to you by telling you something like the total nonsense in your question above. Right?

You're not going to get pregnant from having oral sex, but you have been directly exposed to any STD he has, and, as noted above, STD germs are perfectly happy in your mouth and throat. *Read the item about oral HPV and cancer immediately above if you have not.*

As to whether the person is "clean" or not? "Clean" is often a polite way of saying that the person doesn't have an STD. As we have discussed above, you don't really know, no matter what the person says. As to whether the person washes regularly, your nose will usually tell you.

Question: Is it unhealthy & more likely for someone to catch an STD or STI when they have intercourse while the girl is on their periods.
Can someone get and STI & STD from sharing a vibrator?
(second slip, same girl's neat printing:)

What is TSS & why & how can it kill you?
If someone masterbates & with something & has and STD or STI & whatever thing they masterbated with touched someone else will the other person catch the disease or infection.

Answer(s): Sexual intercourse during menstruation has an equal or greater chance of spreading STDs as intercourse at a time other than menstruation. A number of studies show that HIV is more easily spread during menstrual intercourse, and that all the STD germs and viruses that a person has can be present during menstruation and in the menstrual blood. Again, sex during menstruation does NOT protect you from STDs, and probably makes it easier to catch many STDs. You still have to use a condom.

Sharing sex toys, such as vibrators, can and does transmit STDs from one person to the other. People who share sex toys put a new condom on them and change the condom when the other person uses it. Sorry people, there are no free passes. You have to ALWAYS be smart and protect yourself, or avoid sex altogether—the only truly safe option and the one that no one your age wants to hear.

TSS stands for Toxic Shock Syndrome. It is a sudden and scary infection that showed up about 30 years ago after new types of super-absorbent tampons were introduced to the public. Great idea, but the problem was that they worked TOO well for some people. Since they were *so* absorbent, some women found they didn't need to change the tampon as often, and would in some cases leave it in place for *days*. Bad idea. Various bacteria in the tampon and vagina started feasting on the dead blood, causing sudden, intense infections that could in some cases spread to the blood and other organs. The toxins from the infections could quickly cause organ shutdown and in some cases death before doctors could even figure out what was going on. It's fairly rare and seems to affect people who for whatever reason lack the antibodies to combat staph infections. It is similar to MRSA and other hospital infections one hears about these days. This is why doctors and tampon manufacturers insist that girls and women use the LEAST absorbent tampon that meets their needs, and that they change their tampons regularly no matter what. Symptoms can include fever, diarrhea, vomiting, mental confusion, and skin rashes. If you are using a tampon and develop these symptoms, doctors advise that you remove the tampon and seek medical help immediately. (26)

Question: Can you get an STI without having sex? Is there any STD or STI that a male or female can only get not both sexes?

Answer: Yes to the first, no to the second question. As we have discussed above with herpes, it can be transmitted by kissing. If you have oral HPV, it most likely can be transmitted by kissing as well. Most of the others are pretty difficult to transmit without actual unprotected sex, but again, it's not impossible. HIV/AIDS is commonly transmitted by sharing non-sterile needles in intravenous drug use and can be passed by infected blood being spattered into an eye or an open wound. Genital warts can be transmitted by close skin to skin contact without actual intercourse, as can the skin infection scabies. Transmission from toilet seats and drinking cups is virtually impossible.

As to the second question, both sexes can and do get any and all of the STI/STDs. More importantly, the symptoms vary between the sexes. *Some, like HPV and Herpes can have no symptoms at all for months and years -- or ever for some people -- while they grow and take hold in your bodies and you transmit them unknowingly to others.*

Question: Umm...in the video they said STI's. Is that the same thing as STD's or?

Answer: Yes. STI refers *S*exually *T*ransmitted *I*nfection. STD means *S*exually *T*ransmitted *D*isease. Same thing from a practical standpoint, though some medical practitioners prefer to use STI for someone who has the germ or virus in their body, but has not shown symptoms of the disease yet, and then use STD when they actually have the disease.

Question: What happens if you don't use a condom during sex?

Answer: It depends. Not using a condom means you have had what is known as "unprotected sex." This means that pregnancy and transmittal of any sexually transmitted diseases either person has is possible. If neither person has an STD, and the girl doesn't get pregnant, you've lucked out. But you are betting the life and future of two people on some serious gambles. Either or both people may have an STD and not know it. You hear of cases all the time where a couple has unprotected sex. When the girl doesn't get pregnant, they begin to assume it's okay and they can do so again, and maybe again. It's Russian Roulette. Do you really want to have the rest of both of your lives depend on that kind of luck?

Question: Is they flavor condoms? (English teachers, don't despair! It's not your fault; they are excited and used to texting!!)

Answer: Yes they is. If people want to have oral sex safely, they wear a condom. Flavored condoms make this more pleasant, since the latex rubber itself tastes like, well, rubber. Not great.

Question: How do gay guys get AIDS?

Answer: First, remember, gay guys may be the population most affected by HIV in the United States, but worldwide most people affected by HIV or AIDS are straight people, and almost half are straight women. Sexually, gay men can contract HIV through oral and anal sex. It's relatively harder to transmit it orally, and very easy to do so anally, again for both men and women. Sharing needles for IV drug use (that is, sharing needles while shooting up heroin or other drugs) is also a common way gay and straight people transmit the disease.

Question: I have already had sex and I have AIDS and I didn't tell my girlfriend. What do I do. (Note to reader: This is another of those frustrating questions that I found in the question box weeks later after we had ended Family Life Education. I have no idea who wrote it or if it is for real versus one of those hypotheticals kids like to ask. I really regret not being able to rant on this at length with the kids.)

Answer: The first question is, "Did you have ***unprotected sex?***" Unquestionably, you MUST tell her the truth for all sorts of legal and moral reasons. You simply do not have the right to potentially expose someone to a deadly disease without telling them. Further, under the laws of the state of California, you could be in serious criminal legal trouble if you do not tell a sex partner that you are infected with HIV if you in fact know that you are.

Now, the statement "I have AIDS" covers a lot of ground. In current medical terminology, "having AIDS" means you have the symptoms and diseases that AIDS patients have when HIV has messed up their immune system enough that they start catching all the various diseases and infections that AIDS patients get. I don't believe we have any cases that advanced at this school. However, you can have the HIV virus—and transmit it—without having AIDS symptoms for many years. And, if you and your family know you have the virus, you are most likely already taking the "cocktail" of medicines that suppress the virus. This in turn makes it harder, but by no means impossible, for you to transmit the virus during sex. People who carry the AIDS virus must be absolutely fanatical about safer sex, and you MUST tell your girlfriend that she has been exposed so she can be tested and treated immediately if she has been infected. Again, legally and morally you simply MUST TELL HER NOW. Further, if you really did have unprotected sex without telling the person, sit down and really look at yourself. You let the desire for sex endanger someone else's life and override every decent, moral decision you knew you should make in this situation. You wouldn't ask the question if you didn't already know the answer. You are by no means the first, last, or only person to do this, but please make it the last time for you.

Question: Can you get diseases from being fingered? Can you tell when the condom breaks?

Answer: Like many sexual questions, it's hard to give a straight yes or no answer. Certainly it's pretty unlikely that manual stimulation of the girl will transmit an STD. However, if the guy or the girl herself has touched the guy's penis and come in contact with pre-ejaculate (pre-cum in street language) that is infected with whatever he might have, it can be passed to the girl. Again, not too likely, but it happens.

Then there is the matter of breaking condoms. The problem with a condom that breaks (and they DO break sometimes) is that the people involved are almost always in the midst of intercourse and their minds and not checking on whether the condom is doing its job or not. Their minds are usually very distracted with what they are experiencing and even if "broken condom" crosses their mind, they may finish the sex act before they calm down enough to check, and of course by then it's too late. The rational, problem-solving part of your brain doesn't work too well during sex. So by then the guy has ejaculated, exposing the girl to pregnancy and both people to whatever STDs their partner may have. It can be hard to tell if a condom has broken without pulling out the penis and checking. If you think the condom has broken, you *have to stop and replace it.*

If it does break, you have to consider what pregnancy-preventing measures you may take and should both be checked for STDs unless you already have been checked and neither of you has had unprotected sex with anyone else.

Condoms break. It happens. If you can't face that possibility and deal with it when it happens, you are not ready for sex.

Question: What is a condom for girls and how do you use it?

Answer: The "female condom" is a larger, "inside out" condom type designed to be inserted up into the woman's vagina before intercourse, rather than over a man's penis. The directions on the box are very clear. It covers the outside of the vulva as well providing a barrier in the vagina itself. As such it provides good protection for both the man and the woman.

Question: What is the percent chance of transmitting disease even with use of a condom?
If you have a condum and your having sex. If it doesn't break or fall off can you still get STDs.

Answer: Good questions. Everyone wants a guarantee that nothing bad will happen. That's not real life. The U.S. Government's Center for Disease Control studies show that condoms ***properly and consistently used*** greatly reduce (***but do not eliminate***) the chance of diseases carried in genital fluids like semen and vaginal fluids. These diseases include HIV, chlamydia and hepatitis. However, these same studies show that *while condoms help*, skin contact diseases that may be present in the persons having sex in areas not covered or protected by the condom can and are still transmitted. Such diseases include herpes, HPV, and bacterial diseases like syphilis that can cause sores in places other than the genitals. Condoms still reduce the rate of transmission for these skin contact diseases, but not as much as they help with genital/body fluid transmission. Again, there are no guarantees. The only safe sex is no sex, or a long term, monogamous (that is, an exclusive, no sex with anyone else) sexual relationship with someone who is not infected with disease. (20)

Question: Can we use a balloon as a condom if needed.
Could you use materials other than an actual condom? Why or why not.

Can you replace a condem with a balloon?

Answer: People have used pretty much anything you can imagine as condoms. The earliest ones were actually made of thin leather, and later "lambskin" condoms were made from the intestinal tissue of sheep and other animals. People your age have tried plastic wrap, balloons, and even sandwich bags. **DON'T !**

Here it is again: **IF YOU ARE NOT ABLE TO FACE THE COST OR EMBARRASSMENT OF BUYING REAL, QUALITY CONDOMS, YOU ARE NOT READY FOR SEX. EITHER GROW UP AND DO THE RIGHT THING OR PUT OFF HAVING SEX UNTIL YOU CAN.**

Why am I being so mean? Because this is your life, or rather, the life of everyone involved. It's fun to joke about these alternatives, but it's just that, a joke, not the way to risk your health, your life, and possibly a pregnancy. How much are you willing to pay, or have your parents pay, in the doctor bills, medicines, and complications to your life just because you were too embarrassed, too stupid, too cheap, or too broke to buy condoms? Sure, you may get away with trying these things for a while. Then again, you could have a disaster the first time, and you certainly won't always get away with it. Then what?

Condoms are carefully made to do their job. Good manufacturers spend a lot of time and money on quality control and testing. Even then, condoms can break and fail. However, used properly and carefully, they work very well. Balloons, for starters—at least any that I've seen in stores—are both too *small* and improperly shaped to be condoms. This is another one of those cases where I have to ask, if you *can* get a balloon to fit over your penis, isn't that just really embarrassing? Assuming you could stretch them enough to pull them over your penis (doubtful), they would be so tight that it would painfully strangle the poor thing.

They are not sterile, and they still tear easily. Plastic wrap and sandwich bags, while avoiding the tightness issue, still do not seal around the penis properly and safely like condoms. They can be at best uncomfortable and at worst painful for the people using them, especially the girl.

Question: One time I peed in the morning and some white stuff came out in the end. What is that.

Answer: Well, if you have not had sex with someone else, and if it hasn't happened again, it is almost certainly *not* a symptom of a STD. It probably is some seminal fluid left over from a wet dream you didn't remember you had. If you *have* had sex with someone else, and/or if has happened again, you should have a doctor check you for STDs.

Question: Can a person get an STD from making contact with a toilet seat?

Answer: One of the most basic and common questions in sex ed. The fact is, virtually all STD germs, whether virus or bacteria, are very fragile and die very quickly (in minutes, if not seconds) when removed from the warm, wet confines of human body fluids. That means they just don't last very long on a toilet seat or any place outside the human body. Now, conceivably, if a drop of some body fluid containing STD germs was on a toilet seat, and someone *immediately* sat on the seat, *and* had an open sore of some sort that exactly landed on the drop of germ-containing fluid, some kind of transmission might be possible. You never want to say never in this business, but it's pretty unlikely.

Question: If you have a cut on your penis and then masturbate can you get a disease?

Answer: Well, if the wounded penis doesn't hurt too much to masturbate, you should still wash your hands before and after masturbating. Now, you might make your penis more sore, and possibly encourage an infection in the cut, but for the reasons described above, you're highly unlikely to give yourself an STD by masturbating.

Question: Can you get aids from your own semen?

Answer: Okay, this is one of those where I try desperately not to giggle. You have to understand that if the HIV/AIDS virus is in your semen, you already have the disease, whether you have symptoms or not. It's too late to worry if you will give it to yourself; you already have it. This is one of those times where you have to think about what you are asking.

Question: Are STDs bad?

Answer: Well, when is the last time you heard of a "good" disease? Left untreated, many of them are permanent, disfiguring, fatal, or incurable. Most people would generally describe that as bad. Now, having an STD does not make you a bad person. It may mean you are unlucky, or subject to the wishful thinking, "It can't happen to me because I'm nice/just this one time should be okay/but I really like him/her" nonsense all humans are capable of.

Question: Can medicine treat all STDs?

Answer: No. It's very common for young people to think that we must have medicine and cures for everything in these modern times. We don't, but it's not a simple question. Most of the bacteria-caused STDs can be cured, but it is getting increasingly difficult to do so. Diseases caused by bacteria, like gonorrhea, syphilis, and chlamydia, used to be easily treated with a few days of antibiotic shots or pills. However, like many other bacteria-caused diseases, STD bacteria have evolved resistance to these antibiotics such as penicillin, tetracycline, and the like. We have to continually develop new, stronger, more expensive antibiotics and give them for longer periods of time, sometimes months, to wipe out an infection. Some species are almost impossible to treat. There are some common strains of chlamydia, for example that are almost incurable even with the latest antibiotics.

Antibiotics *do not work on any disease caused by a virus*, and none of the viral diseases like herpes, HIV, and genital warts are curable. We *have* developed some medicines that control and limit the disease. Valtrex ™ can inhibit the herpes virus, stopping outbreaks for months, sometimes years, and can shorten outbreaks when they happen. But you always have the virus, and you can always transmit it.

For genital warts, caused by the human papillomavirus, there is now a vaccine called Gardacil™ that can prevent women and men from getting several of the *most common species* of this virus. However, there is no cure once you have the virus, *and the vaccine does not protect against all forms of the virus.* Recent research has shown that an increasing number of mouth and throat cancers *in both men and women* are caused by the human papillomavirus, just as it can cause cervical cancer in women. The presence of HPV in the mouth and throat means that *men and women are picking it up through unprotect oral sex.* Doctors and gynecologists have been recommending that young women get the Gardacil ™ vaccine as early as 10 years of age. *It now seems that boys should get it as well, and you may notice that the latest Gardacil ads on TV now feature boys as well as girls. As always, doctors should be consulted.*

There are dozens of treatment medicines for HIV/AIDS these days, the oldest being AZT, and a number of related drugs that suppress the virus, often to levels where it can no longer be detected in the blood. *But again, the disease is incurable.* You always have it, and the virus often mutates and evolves resistance to existing drugs, requiring the development of new drugs. The disease often eventually kills the patient in many parts of the world, though many with access to Western medicine are now living decades with the disease, and we don't know yet how long a "healthy" person who contracts the disease can expect to live. Magic Johnson certainly looks like a healthy guy and he has had the disease for nearly 30 years. He is also wealthy, was a top athlete, and can afford to get the very best treatment. The available medicines are improving, but the best still usually require the patient to take three different pills through the day to be effective, every day of the patient's life. They are not cheap, and over a lifetime can cost tens if not hundreds of thousands of dollars that the patient, depending on their health insurance, may have to pay at least part of. They are not always easy on the body either, causing various side effects.

There has been a huge worldwide effort and billions of dollars spent to find a cure or a vaccine for HIV, and other than the family of drugs that can control and inhibit the disease, there has been little success. The virus is incredibly adaptable and continually evolves ways around what look to be promising medicines and vaccines. There are new avenues of research opening up, but nothing even close to success yet.

Question: If you have a wart on your penis, and it goes in the vagina can the girl get an STD?

Answer: As noted above, it depends. If the wart on your penis is caused by the Human papillomavirus (HPV) then that can easily be transmitted by contact with the vagina. Regular warts don't usually show up on the genitals and are harder to transmit, but it's certainly possible.

Question: How many STD's are there?

Answer: Lots. There are couple dozen common ones, and more exotic ones depending on the part of the world where you are having unprotected sex. Keep in mind, that when someone says they got "chlamydia," that means it could be any one of dozens of species of that bacteria that infect people, some of which are easily cured, while other species are ***almost impossible*** to eradicate even with the most modern antibiotics. If you count all the various species and mutations of modern STDs, you could well be talking about hundreds if not thousands of kinds.

Question: Can you have more than 1 STD at a time like herpes and Aid. Do they create a super herpe.

Answer: STD germs are willing to share. From their standpoint, there is lots of room in your body for everyone. You can have multiple species of herpes and any other STD germ, and lots of different kinds at one time. They don't care.

Question: Can you get hepatitis from kissing?

Answer: Almost never. Hepatitis A, B and C are virus-caused diseases of the blood that can damage the liver. Hep A is spread by poor personal hygiene and/or poor local sanitation. Contact with contaminated feces is the source of infection. Hep B can be contracted through unprotect sex or blood/body fluid contact through shared needles from drugs or poor hospital hygiene. Hepatitis C is also spread by blood/body fluid exchange but is difficult to contract sexually. None of the three kinds of hepatitis are transmitted by kissing.

Question: What is a blue waffle?

Answer: "Blue waffle disease" appears to be a recently-coined term for the appearance of a vagina/vulva where a woman has a severe, chronic, untreated vaginal infection and/or yeast infection or multiple infections. The result is extreme discomfort, discharge, odor, and a pale or bluish tinge to the damaged and diseased vulva and vaginal tissue. This condition is usually the result of someone not taking good care of their sexual health for a long time.

Question: What's a yeast infection?

Answer: Yeasts are a huge group of mostly microscopic organisms that are part of the fungus family along with things like mushrooms and mold. There are thousands of species living in all sorts of places. Most people know that yeasts are important in making bread, cheese, beer, and wine, as well as many other biological and chemical processes. And some live in the vagina. Now the normal chemistry of the vagina keeps them from getting out of hand, but if something gets out of balance for any number of reasons, they can multiply and cause a "yeast infection" in the vagina. It can and does happen whether you've had sex or not.

This is not normally dangerous, but they can be very uncomfortable, causing severe burning and itching sensations in the vagina, as well as a lot of smelly discharge. Not fun. They are easily cured with any number of over the counter drugs available at the store. Still, if you have a yeast infection for the first time, it's best to see a doctor to get it checked out rather than automatically buying an over the counter cure.

Question: What are crabs?

Answer: Crabs are a kind of lice (small insects) that prefer to live in pubic hair rather than the hair on your head. They suck the blood of their host like fleas and lice, and their bites can be itchy like flea bites. They are passed by people having sex, and condoms don't help, because they live in pubic hair, not on or in the penis or vagina. They can also be transmitted by sharing a bed with someone who has them, whether you have sex with that person or not. They can be eliminated by the use of prescription shampoos and ointments designed to kill them.

VARIOUS SEX ACTS

Note to Reader: As you might expect, this one is often the biggest pile of question slips each year. There is so much street "knowledge" passed around, so much they have seen or heard about from the porn industry, that the questions and the titles and the acts asked about continually evolve each year. It is a fertile and ever growing topic...

Question: If you have an erection and a girl gives you a BJ, can she choke?
If you are giving a guy a BJ, could your throat get clogged from all the cum?
Can you choke on cumm?
Can a girl die from choking on a penis?
Is it bad to put a penis down your throat?
Can a girl die from chocking on a penis

Answer: Well first, most assuredly, if a girl is giving you a BJ (the technical term for this kind of oral sex is fellatio) you will shortly have an erection, if you don't already, so that part is kind of a given. As to choking: if the penis is shoved down her throat, the gag reflex will cause her to choke, of course. Most people learn to avoid this. If you are asking if she will choke on the semen if you ejaculate, again, it somewhat depends on her gag reflex and/or whether some of the semen goes "down the wrong pipe." However, dying is unlikely. Keep in mind that the actual amount of semen in most ejaculations is about a teaspoon, so the amount of semen itself is not likely to choke or drown anyone. That doesn't mean that that everyone likes the taste or having it squirted in their mouth or down their throat. Most girls/women surprisingly don't greatly enjoy the choking part of oral sex, of course, and most people learn to avoid this with practice and out of consideration and politeness. Again, by definition, these questions state that you are having unprotected oral sex, which means both people are exposed to whatever STIs either person has in their mouth and/or penis.

Question: Is it healthy to swallow your partner's ejaculation?
I have eaten spirm before. Is that bad?

Answer: There are two parts to this answer. First, if someone ejaculates in your mouth, you have had unprotected sex with that guy. (I know, I keep saying this. That's because you need to keep hearing it because in your little trusting heart of teenage hearts you really want to believe that since you are a nice person therefore the person you are with must be a nice person, nothing bad can happen so it's okay to do anything because bad things don't happen to nice people... but they do...) That means you can get whatever STD(s) he may have in *your* mouth and *your* throat. If he has no STDs then you are okay. Of course, you know he has no STDs, right, because he has been tested so he knows, and he's been totally honest with himself and with you, right? Besides, nice guys (the only kind you would have sex with) don't get STDs and never lie about it, right? You have to keep that in mind, and sexually active adults often use condoms even for oral sex for just that reason. Keep in mind that if you use a condom for oral sex he also doesn't ejaculate in your mouth, but in the condom, which may people would say is a plus.

The second part of the answer is that in and of itself, ejaculate is not harmful to swallow. It is high in protein, and can be considered nutritious from that standpoint. Not normally a first choice for a high protein diet, however...

Question: Is it bad to touch a girl's vagina, or lick it?
What's a dental dam?

Answer: Bad? No. Both of those things are pretty basic sex acts between males and females. However, the same warning about unprotected sex applies as it does for oral sex with a guy. If you have unprotected oral sex with a girl, you are orally exposing yourself to whatever STDs she may have down there. If she has no STDs, there is no problem. But as nice a girl as she is, you don't really know that, and she may not know herself.

This is why many sexually active adults use what is called a "dental dam." If you have had fillings or other extended tooth work at a dentist, you may have been aware of the dentist stretching a thin piece of rubber over the rest of your mouth to protect it and the tooth he is working on from germs and debris. This sheet of rubber is called a "dental dam," and many responsible, sexually active adults use it when they have oral sex with a woman they don't know well. They place the thin rubber sheet over the vulva while having oral sex with the woman.

Which leads back to the theme of this book. You can't be innocently clueless in today's sex world. You have to be aware of the responsibilities to yourself and your partner if you are going to have sex outside of a permanent, committed relationship. Or, wait until you *are* ready to deal with these responsibilities.

Question: What does it mean to pop a girl's cherry?
What does the term pop your cherry mean?

Answer: "Popping your cherry" is an old (it's older than my late dad) term for losing your virginity, or having sex for the first time. It refers to the fact that it is very common during a girl's first sexual intercourse to tear the hymen, a small membrane that partially closes the opening of the vagina. This causes some pain and a small amount of bleeding, hence the "popped cherry" reference. Very often, this pain and bleeding has more to do with the hurried, and not always careful, enthusiasm of young men when they first have sex with a girl, since it is common for both parties to be virgins and not be totally clear on what they are doing. Patience and consideration can go a long way...

Question(s): What is a virgin?
What is mooning?
What is 69?
What is mono? (note, these four were all one question slip)
In "69", which is the "6"and which is the "9".
Are you still a virgin if a guy has sex with titties like tity sex?

Answer(s): Quite a list. A virgin, as noted above, is a person, male or female, who has never had sexual intercourse before.

Now, this definition can be tricky, since it traditionally means that you have never had penis in vagina intercourse – and in most peoples' minds that's what it still means to be a virgin. So, people who have avoided penis-in-vagina sex often claim to be virgins, even if they have actively engaged in manual, oral, anal, or yes, titty sex. This is now known as the "Bill Clinton defense." Wishful thinking and self-deception again. If you are engaging in activities where you are touching and stimulating someone else's sex organs, or someone is doing it to you, you are having sex. If you can still claim with a straight face, "yes daddy, I'm still a virgin," because you have not had penis-in-vagina sex, suit yourself, but you now know the truth.

"Mooning" is another old term for dropping your pant(ie)s and showing your butt to someone or a group of people as a joke or insult. Not much more to it.

"69" is a term for mutual oral sex. The French used to be given credit for it, mostly because the French used to get credit for most things sexual or "dirty" in the old days (like "French kissing") because of their liberal cultural attitude toward sex, and also because the French pronunciation of the number 69, soix-ant-neuf, sounds so cool and sexy. To understand the term "69," picture two people giving each other oral sex at the same time. Their bodies would be curved so that they resemble the number 69. You will have to decide for yourself who is the 6 and who is the 9. It depends on how you spin the numbers around, doesn't it?

"Mono," or mononucleosis, is a viral disease caused by the Epstein-Barr virus and sometimes, the CMV or cytomegalovirus. Its symptoms can include a high fever, severe sore throat, swollen glands and tonsils, and an overall tiredness and weakness. The symptoms start four to six weeks after exposure and can last weeks or even months. Mononucleosis can cause, in some cases, a small organ in your abdomen called the spleen to swell and sometimes burst, requiring hospitalization. In the great majority of cases, however, rest and acetaminophen are all that is needed. There is no medicine that cures it, just time and rest. For some reason, when small children get it, the symptoms are mild and often go unnoticed. Adults are almost always immune whether they ever got it or not, leaving teenagers to be most affected. It's famously called the "kissing disease" because that is a common way that it is transmitted among young people. Once you have the virus, it stays with you for life. It is usually dormant in your body, but sometimes activates, causing no symptoms, but making it much easier to transmit. If you have mono, you should seriously avoid kissing or sharing drinking cups, eating utensils, lipstick/chapstik, toothbrushes, and the like.

Question: Can a guy fit his head in a girl's vagina?
Can you fit a human head in a vagina?

Answer: Really? Seriously? No. This question is almost certainly because of confusion about another old term for oral sex, "giving head." I'm sure it's entirely possible for a 14 year old's imagination to run with this term and assume that there must be some way that if you are "giving head" you are putting your head in a girl's vagina. Uh, no... Even if you wanted to try, girls and women have the good sense to put a stop to such things.

Question: How do you give a blow job?
What is a blow job, a hand job and giving head?

Answer: We handled "giving head" above. Keep in mind this is not a "how to" class. A blow job is another term for oral sex, specifically, putting one person's mouth on someone's penis. Don't know where the "blow" part came from, because there's no blowing involved, other than it probably looked to someone like you were playing some kind of wind instrument. A "hand job" is just a term for using one's hand(s) to stimulate or masturbate someone else to orgasm. Usually it refers to specifically using your hands on someone else's penis.

Question: What is eating out?
My brother said he ate someone out --
what is that?

Answer: It's a common slang term for oral sex on a woman, that is, stimulating the woman's clitoris/vulva with the mouth/tongue. Hopefully, no actual eating takes place. The scientific term is "cunnilingus."

Question: What is shagging?

Answer: Shagging is yet another in the seemingly endless English slang terms for having sex.

Question: What's a douchebag?

Answer: It used to be very common for women to douche, which is French for "bath." Specifically, it refers to bathing or washing out the vagina, often after sex. Doctors now recommend against this, as it does more harm than good to the chemistry of the vagina. A douchebag was typically a small rubber bag sort of like a hot water bottle, with a little hose and nozzle that was inserted into the vagina to rinse it out. It has become a slang term for a guy who is a jerk, low-life, loser, tool, etc.

Question: After like 3 hours would the penis stop having an erection? And, could the penis or the vagina stop coming?
What happens if you have a boner for a long time?

Answer: The average duration of an erection for a healthy young man is 35-50 minutes. Young men can go longer; older men, often less time. If you go three hours without ejaculation, it's unlikely that you will have a full erection that entire time, but rather the erection will at least partly come and go (no pun intended... well maybe). As the erectile dysfunction ads say, if you have an erection that goes more than four hours, you need immediate medical help, because the whole time you have an erection, there is little or no blood circulating through the penis because the blood is trapped there, making you hard. Going that long without the oxygen carried by circulating blood can start to kill the penile tissue, and no one wants that. So, almost certainly, you will lose your erection at some point in this three hour time period, and/or you will have an ejaculation, which will cause the erection to go away quickly.

As to whether the penis or vagina can stop coming, that's more complicated. Males almost universally lose their erection quickly after ejaculation and have to have some downtime between erections and ejaculations. Even for teenagers and young men, this rest time after ejaculation is usually at least 15 minutes to a half hour, though some highly-aroused young men have only partially lost erections, gotten them back, and continued to have sex, followed by another ejaculation. It doesn't happen often, and if it doesn't happen to you, don't worry. Some young men can have erections and ejaculations several times a day, but it gets more difficult each time, and the desire to do so often drops off a lot after a couple times. Usually, the time between erections and ejaculations gets longer each time one tries to get aroused. Further, alcohol or drug use, lack of rest, stress, or distractions in your life can make any of this difficult or impossible.

As with most things that have to do with sex, it's more complicated for women. Unlike men, where it's erection, ejaculation, rest, and then maybe do it again, women have a huge range of orgasmic possibilities, and it can be different each time they have a sexual experience that leads to orgasm, as well as being different for each woman.

Some women have great difficulty reaching orgasm at all, though nowadays with all the self-help books and sex toys, it seems reasonable that most women learn to get there at least some of the time. Remember, to some extent, sexual activity is also a physical skill that you can learn and improve, starting from whatever ability you were born with, like any other physical activity, skill, or sport. Usually reaching orgasm gets easier as women gain self-knowledge and mature from their teens into their twenties. Some have one great big exhausting orgasm and, like men, need to rest and recover before they do it again, or they may find that their clitoris/vulva is too sensitive immediately after orgasm to be stimulated any more. Some can continue to have successive orgasms, perhaps with a couple small ones leading up to a big one, after which they need to stop. Some can almost continually have orgasm after orgasm once they get started until exhaustion and/or sore sex organs make them stop. Sometimes, it just doesn't happen for them, no matter what they or their partner do. The thing is, many women will experience any or all of these possibilities at some point in their life; that is, no orgasm, difficulty reaching orgasm, one big one, a few together, several, or many. Furthermore, each of these experiences may be perfectly satisfying at that time, or they may feel inadequate. Usually, one pattern emerges as normal and satisfying for them, with the other possibilities out there depending on their relationship with their partner, their age, stress, distractions, self-image at the time, their hormone levels, and the time of the month. So, with women, anything is possible, and the reminder that normal is what's normal for you is more true than ever when you are talking about how often a woman can have an orgasm.

Question: Does it hurt to have sex?

Answer: For guys, as a rule, no, unless some disastrous accident/injury happens. For girls and women, the same should be true. The fact is, if it hurts, you are doing something wrong and you should stop whatever it is you are doing – it shouldn't hurt. Now, having said that, the first time a girl has intercourse, the hymen can get stretched or torn, and there can be some bleeding and pain associated with that. However, even in this case, the pain and bleeding often has much more to do with the hurried, over-eager, and sometimes less-than-sensitive enthusiasm of the young male partner. With patience, consideration, and some effort to resist the normal young male impulse to go at it full speed, the first penetration can be much less traumatic – and indeed pleasurable, as it is supposed to be. No guarantees here, often the first few times aren't that great for most women, but it obviously gets better.

This is part of the maturity issue of being ready for sex. Sex is not something you "do" to someone. It is an activity where two people give each other something very special, and if both of you are not ready to deal with the care and consideration of the other person's feeling, safety, and needs, you are not ready for this. There is too much at stake. Very often, girl's early sexual experiences are what they *do for boys*, or what boys do *to* them, not anything that could be called real shared sex or love-making. Many boys expect sex, and expect girls to "give" it to them, and many girls think they have to "give" sex to get or keep a boyfriend.

If girls let it be that way, that's how it will be for them. That's being used, and that's not how it is supposed to work.

Question: What is Doggy style?

Answer: If you have ever seen dogs, or any other four-legged animal for that matter, have sex, that's doggy style. The woman kneels in front, and the man enters her vagina from behind. Not the same as butt sex.

Question: How do adults usually have sex?
What position feels the best?

Answer: Pretty much the same way everybody else does, but hopefully with thought, consideration of the other person's needs and feelings, attention to safer sex, and a clear understanding of what is involved.

As to sexual positions, that's only limited by the human imagination and a couple's willingness to experiment. There are whole books filled with dozens, if not hundreds of positions, the most famous being the centuries old text from India called the *Kama Sutra*. Most people go through a phase of trying a lot of them, only to find that while it may be fun to play around with different positions, many end up being more athletic than sexually satisfying. But everyone has favorites.

Question: Does sex take a lot of energy?
Is more work for girl or man (sex)?
When you have sex, why do you get hot and sweaty?

Answer: Sex, depending on the position and how long it takes either or both people to reach orgasm, can be a pretty energetic activity. Because of that, you can in fact get hot and sweaty, even from just being sexually aroused. That's why people who are sexually attractive are described as being "hot." That's why people who have heart conditions have to be careful about sex, and also why it is considered a healthy part of an adult couple's life. Whether it is more work for one person or the other also depends on what you are doing. Certainly either partner can take charge and/or you can choose a position that puts most of the physical effort on one person or the other. All part of the fun.

Question: What is the point of oral sex? And how exactly does it work?
Is oral sex good for the soul?

Answer: Well, it works just fine, and that's the point of it. It is another way to have sex with someone. Oral sex is just what the name implies: it's sex with the mouth, specifically using the mouth and tongue to stimulate someone else's sex organs, whether it's the male penis or the female clitoris/vulva. It's like any other sexual experience in that it can be great, not so great, or whatever... Questions of how it benefits the soul are best left to others more qualified than I.

Question: How can pornstars fit so much down their throat?

Answer: You must remember that porn starts are in fact highly trained and experienced sexual athletes. They perform more sex acts in a week of work than many people do in years of normal life, more than some people do in a lifetime. Many porn starts learn through practice to suppress their gag reflex so that they can push a penis down their throat without throwing up. Of course, they threw up many times learning how. Something to aspire to...

Question: When you have sex sometimes people get orgasims why does this occur?
What is the peak of orgasims?
Why do women have orgasims?
What is an ejaculation?

Answer: An orgasm – o-r-g-a-s-m – is kind of the point of having sex from the pleasure and reproductive standpoint. Physically, an orgasm is somewhat similar in both sexes. For males, orgasm is ejaculation. It involves a series of usually several strong, pleasurable contractions of the muscles around the prostate gland that squirt the semen out the erect penis. This reflex is set off by stimulation of the penis and particularly the head of the penis, though simply being strongly sexually aroused or excited can cause it.

For women, orgasm is multiple, pleasurable contractions of muscles of the vagina and uterus usually set off by stimulation of the clitoris, and sometimes the G-spot, or both. Again, a state of extreme sexual arousal without actual physical stimulation can cause orgasm for some women. For both sexes, the physical contractions are usually accompanied by spasmodic contractions of many muscles of the body and strong emotional, mental, and overall body sensations of extreme pleasure and well-being, followed by a period of intense pleasurable relaxation and drowsiness.

From the reproductive standpoint, orgasm and the anticipation of the pleasure of orgasm makes people want to have sex, which makes having babies more likely. It also appears to have a role in bonding two people together for the purpose of raising children. Studies show that the brains of people who have sex and orgasms and orgasms with each other release the pleasure chemicals called endorphins, natural pleasure-inducing drugs your body makes that make you like each other even more.

Question: Can you die if a guy's condom comes off during sex and it gets pushed in? Can a female condom get pushed in to far and could you die?

Answer: Look, it's not *that* unusual for a condom to come off, especially if it's not put on properly, or sometimes if the man loses his erection inside the vagina. I'm sure that some unfortunate girl somewhere who didn't know her body and what was going on died of an infection resulting from leaving a condom in her vagina. In the enthusiasm of sexual intercourse, it is possible to not realize that the condom has slipped off, and it can get pushed up to the top of the vagina. If it's cluelessly left there for a long period of time, say days or weeks, it is possible that a nasty and possibly fatal infection could start from bacteria that find a place to live in the folds of the condom and vaginal tissue.

However, this should never happen, and the whole issue should not be a big deal (other than that the "protected" sex you just had is now no longer protected, and all those sperm are swimming past the crumpled condom looking to get into the uterus and points beyond, and you are now exposed to whatever STDs your partner had) if the girl is at all aware of her body. The vagina is not some bottomless cavern where things disappear never to be seen again. Most women can reach their fingers up and get the "lost" condom with a bit of effort. Many times just standing up and going to the bathroom will shake the condom down, making it reachable. If not, your partner may have to help and see if he can get it out by *gently (!)* reaching in with his fingers to see if he can get it. If for some reason this is not possible, then a quick trip to the doctor will be needed in the next day or so at most to avoid the possibility of an infection. At the same time, both partners should be tested for STDs, and a pregnancy test should be taken by the woman.

All this is even less likely with a female condom. They are larger than a regular male condom, and they fit over the outside of the vulva. It's pretty hard to push them all the way in, and it's much easier to get them out if somehow you do get it pushed up there.

I'm going to say it again (and again!). If you find dealing with these possibilities too gross, embarrassing, or icky, that is: putting the condom on right, retrieving it if it does get lost, and getting medical help so that both partners are protected, then you are not ready for sex. These things happen. It's part of having sex, and it's fine to say "I'm still a kid, however grown up I want to feel. I don't need to deal with this at this point in my life."

Question: Does the vaginal grow or open a little when you have sex?

Answer: Yes, it does, quite a lot. As the woman gets aroused, the vagina's muscular and erectile tissue cause it to get longer and relax and open compared to its normal resting condition. This, along with the lubrication the vaginal walls produce, makes sexual intercourse easier. Lubrication, or "getting wet," is the female equivalent of getting an erection.

Questions: Can you get stuck in sex?
Can your penis get stuck in a girl's vagina? If so, dose (my god, spelling!!) it have to be surgicly removed?
What if your penis gets stuck in the girl's hmmmm....?

Is it true that the penis could get stuck in the vagina?
Can a penis get stuck in a vagina during intercourse?

Answer: Yes, it happens, but not very often, and *very few people* ever experience it. Keep in mind that the vagina is a muscle. It is possible for it to cramp like the cramps or "charley horse" you can get in your leg muscles. This means that, for some reason, the muscles can contact strongly and involuntarily during intercourse, clamping down on the penis. The vagina can do this strongly enough that the man cannot pull his penis out, and the two people can be stuck together. While it may sound funny, it's not comfortable or funny to the people it happens to. Usually, a combination of the cramp passing and the man losing his erection lets the two people separate, but sometimes paramedics have to be called and a muscle relaxant shot given to make it possible for the vagina to relax and release the penis. I've never heard of surgery being required. This is not something to spend a lot of time worrying about.

So much fear out there...

Question: If a guy is eating a girl out can his tounge get stuck if it goes in to far?

Answer: Someone has an exaggerated impression of the size of their tongue. No, the tongue is neither long enough, nor fat enough, to get stuck, even in a cramped vagina.

Question: Why do girls like to give "BJ"?
Can you get prego by givin a blo job?
Can you get pregnet through anal sex (see below) or oral sex?

Why do guys like girls to do oral sex on there pennis so much?

Answer: Well, some do, some don't. Like everything else about humans, it varies, and it depends. Some girls and women really like giving oral sex because most men and boys like it a lot, it gives the woman control of the situation, and some just like doing it, period. It has the advantage for the woman in that they can't get pregnant, *and* boys like it a lot. Other women hate doing it because they don't like the sensations or tastes, or they choke or feel forced or obliged to provide oral sex, and like most things we feel we *have* to do, it's not much fun then.

By the way, Prego™ is a brand of spaghetti sauce.

Guys like oral sex, well, because it's sex, and it just happens to be oral. Let me repeat, it's sex. Most guys like sex, pretty much any way they can get it. Oral can be very intense, it doesn't cause pregnancy, and it often fulfills a lot of male fantasies about sex.

Question: If a girl gives you a hand job and you ejaculate in her face, would that make a bad first impression?

Answer: How to answer this? If your first impression of each other is a hand job, you probably both deserve whatever happens, including getting squirted in the face and the inevitable bad impression. And, if you really need to ask this question, please sign your name next time so we can make sure all the girls know what idiot to avoid for hand jobs or anything else.

Question: Is it physically possible to suck your own penis?

Answer: For normally constructed guys, sorry, no, you are just not that flexible. There are some highly flexible, "double jointed" individuals who can reportedly pull it off, but they are rare. Too bad, it would make so many young guys so happy....

Question: What is double penetration?
What is double penetration, what is triple penetration? (guy handwriting)
What is double penitration? (perfect girl handwriting, with cute little circles for dotting the "i's")
Is it possible for a girl to have a penis in all three holes (vagina, anus and mouth)

Answer: Double penetration normally means multiple partner sex where someone, usually a woman, has two penises in her, penetrating any two of the possible three holes: her vagina, anus, or mouth. From that, you can see that triple penetration is a penis in the mouth, anus, and vagina.

Question: Can you have sex under water?

Answer: Yes, but... This is one of those things that most people find not to be nearly as enjoyable or cool as it sounds. It's certainly possible, but the big problem is that the water rinses away the woman's vaginal lubrication, and most guys find it hard to maintain a useable erection if the water is cool at all. Both of those problems make it difficult at best for many people who try it. There are also potential health risks for the woman, in that water can be pushed into her uterus by the sexual thrusting, and this can cause infections. We are not whales.

Question: How come people do it in public?

Answer: Why do people do any of the things they do that don't make sense to us? Some people like doing it where they might be seen or caught. It makes it more exciting for them.

Question: What do penis's taste like?

Answer: Couldn't tell you myself. They are made of tender skin, so they probably taste like other tender skin areas of your body. Cleanliness, what foods you have eaten, and other factors all can affect the smell and taste down there.

Question: Can the vagina rip if the penis is too big?
Could a women tear her vagina if she tried to put something to big in it? And could something like a penny get stuck up there?

Answer: In normal sexual intercourse, no. Again, the vagina can pass a baby, so really a penis is not a big deal, whatever it size. However, if it is the first sexual intercourse with a virgin girl, and if she is not fully aroused, lubricated, and relaxed, it is possible to do some significant, painful damage. Women who are raped, that is, forcibly penetrated, are obviously not relaxed, aroused, or lubricated, and they often suffer some tearing and damage to the vagina. Most women have a pretty good idea of how big an object they can put in their vagina.

Now, a penny? In the vagina? Why, how? Again, the vagina is not bottomless. It's only four or so inches long, so a penny should be retrievable. If, however, you have a penny up there for some reason, and can't get it out, you must see a doctor, because it probably will cause an infection if left there.

Question: After giving a girl a superman, how do you get the bed sheet of the girls back?

Answer: Normally I wouldn't even answer a lame question like this. No doubt it's from the same guy who asked about the hand job in the face, and reflects the same lack of thought and class. That's the main reason I'll answer it, because girls need to be aware of what's out there in *some* members of the male half of the species.

First, a Superman has got to be the lamest sex act ever imagined by some frat boy who wants to get even with all the girls who won't have sex with him because he's a clueless tool. It assumes you are having sex from behind (doggy style) with a girl who is so drunk she's basically unconscious, *because no conscious girl in her right mind would put up with anything this stupid and humiliating.* That fact that she is unconscious alone makes it *quite possibly an act of rape under current law.* The idea is that you pull out of her vagina and ejaculate onto her back, followed by throwing the bed sheet over her back. Since the girl is unconscious, the sheet will remain there and the semen will dry, causing it to be stuck to her back like a cape when she does wake up, giving it the act its name.

So, let's lets recap: 1) You are having sex with an unconscious or nearly unconscious girl (now young guys will have sex with anything, but how much fun is a comatose girl?), making the act quite likely to be legally defined as rape; 2) You pull *out* of her vagina just so you can ejaculate on her back which means you are probably not using a condom; *and,* 3) You throw the bed sheet over the unconscious girl because you think having it get stuck on her back is more fun than having sex with someone who might actually enjoy it with you; and 4) You think semen is superglue, which means you are just dumb, and not worthy of passing your genes on to children someday.

To finish this discussion, please understand that the sheet will peel loose with little if any discomfort, or at worst with a little help from a damp sponge.

And girls wonder why their parents worry about them going to parties...

Question: What is beastiality?

Answer: It's the term for having sex with animals, assuming you can find one with the poor self-image and bad taste to have sex with you. Both men and women have been known to do such things. Like I said above, young guys will put it in *anything*... Obviously, not their proudest moment.

Question: What is porn and what do they do?

Answer: "Porn" is short for pornography, which is literally translates from Greek as "harlot (prostitute) writing" or "writing about harlots," which in turn is the term for any literature, video, or art form that specifically and graphically has to do with describing or showing sex in all its forms. It can, depending on who is describing or defining it, be anything from an artistic nude painting, to erotic stories and novels, to videos of things that turn most people's stomach, to everything in between. Historically, it has referred to erotic art works, novels and stories of sex, then photos, movies, and video tapes, down to the online streaming of porn videos today. When you say "porn" today, most people think of the huge pornographic video business that is produced for online viewing over the Internet showing people having sex.

Question: What is a "Dirty Sanchez?"

Answer: We're really not going to go there. Aside from the racial and political incorrectness of it all, let's just say it involves anal sex and finger painting with poop. More drunken fratboy class...

Which leads us to our special section on one of the current middle school obsessions:

THE FASCINATION WITH ANAL (OR BUTT) SEX

One year it was the "chode" that they couldn't hear enough about; the next year it was butt sex. This act, as distasteful as it is for some, has become more and more accepted in much of the straight population. Of course the porn industry is part of the reason (again parents **many, many of you parents need to review and update your internet access control software)**. It's clear that many young people are getting access to porn on line directly or through older siblings, relatives and friends, and anal sex is a staple of porn video. In turn, porn is kind of a fact of life for many teenage boys nowadays. Of course teenagers are perfectly capable of discovering anal sex on their own or through word of mouth.

But porn is not the only reason anal sex is becoming a more common aspect of sex, even with teenagers. If you want to remain a technical virgin ("Honest Daddy, no penis-in-vagina sex for me!"), want to avoid pregnancy, and don't want to *always* have manual or oral sex, it's kind of the only remaining option. Anal sex is hardly new with this generation – it's referred to in texts as ancient as the Bible. The ancient Greeks practiced and preferred it with both straight and gay partners – hence the old term "going Greek." It was, of course, known to the Romans and pretty much any other culture, many of whom abhorred it officially while others were more accepting. Many people may shudder at it, but it wouldn't stay around for millennia if a large number people, *both men and women*, didn't enjoy it. But, make no mistake, it is very high risk activity, especially for young, over-eager and inexperience practitioners. It's still one of the most common ways HIV is transmitted, and the delicacy of the anal/rectal area makes it a location for all sorts of inadvertent, embarrassing, and hard-to-clear-up injuries and infections, as well as the entire list of STDs. Experienced, patient, and mature practitioners of anal sex who do all the right things manage the act without problems, but anal sex it a hot bed of Murphy's law possibilities for the young and the dumb. Soooooo...

Question: What's the deal with anal sex?

Answer: Anal sex is intercourse where the penis is inserted into the anus and rectum, the lower end of the intestines where poop comes out. Many people are horrified by the very thought of such an act, but others hugely enjoy the sensations. It is certainly much harder to get pregnant with anal sex, but not impossible, as we noted in the section on pregnancy and childbirth. From your standpoint as teenagers, it's very high risk activity. Let us count the ways:

1. The vagina is actually quite tough, stretchy, and self-lubricating, because it is designed for sex and accommodating things as big as babies.
2. The anus and rectum have none of these handy characteristics. They are small, tight, non-lubricating, with delicate and easily-torn tissue that stretches reluctantly at best.

3. Because of this delicacy, it is easily injured, and it is ***very easy to transmit <u>all</u> the STIs (you name it, it's easier to get anally)*** through the thin, easily-torn tissues.

4. If one does injure, that is tear, the delicate tissue though anal intercourse, the massive load of bacteria present in the feces (poop!) that pass through the anal and rectal area can make it easier for these injuries to become infected. Most teenagers find these injuries and infections almost impossibly embarrassing to ask about or explain to a parent or doctor, so they often go untreated until they require hospitalization and/or surgery to correct. This same high bacteria load makes it very easy for unprotected penises to pick up urethra and urinary tract infections.

5. **Therefore, it is at least as important to use a condom for anal sex as it is for vaginal sex**, a huge disappointment for teenagers who hope anal sex means not needing that pesky condom.

6. All of these issues are made worse by the naturally hurried, over-excited, and enthusiastic approach to sex any young person, male or female, has. Usually, teenagers have limited time for sex, limited privacy at best, and hormonal overdrive that makes a patient and gentle approach almost impossible.

7. The anus is really close to the vagina. The semen that goes in the anus has to come out at some time. If some of it makes that short trip to the vagina, pregnancy is possible, however unlikely. It happens.

8. Those of you watching porn on line—the source of most of these questions, right guys? – can get the idea that butt sex is just like regular/straight/vaginal sex. I mean, that's the way is looks in the porn videos, right? Just jam it in there (generally not good for the vagina either) and go to it whether it's a vagina or an anus...

Uh.... No.

First, those women are in fact professional, trained sexual athletes who know exactly what they are doing and spend HOURS warming up, relaxing and stretching the anal/rectal muscles, getting enemas (you know, hosing out your butt by putting a little nozzle in your anus that's attached to a rubber bag of warm water, squeeze the water into your butt, and then sit on the toilet to get rid of the water and hopefully all the poop up there so it doesn't ruin the movie...) and lubricating the anus *a lot* before anal scenes are shot. Usually the performers are careful about what they eat the day before too, so there is less poop to contend with. Of course, *none* of this lengthy preparation is in the porno video itself... It's a *lot* of preparation just so you can convince yourself any girl would be thrilled to bend over and let you have a go at her anus... The fact is, while undeniably many women enjoy it, most women just don't find anal sex to be that much fun or enjoyable, and you can't blame them for wondering, "I have a perfectly good vagina, *why* would you want to put it in my butt!?"

Everything about anal sex requires more thought, care, and patience than vaginal sex, not less. Forethought, care and patience are all things NOT associated with teenagers, especially teenage boys. Be honest people, you know this is true.

Question: If you are having anal sex, can you get poop on your penis?
If you have anal sex will your dong come out all poopy?

Answer: Yes you can get poop on your penis from anal sex (see above).

Question: Is it possible to kill a girl by having anal sex if you have a big enough penis?
So if that guy with that huge 13 inch dick puts it in a very small person ass could something on the inside get squished or broken?

Answer: A true guy **question:** sex, violence, and a big penis. This is another one I wouldn't answer except as a warning to girls that there is a significant portion of the guys out there who think this way. For some of them, sex is about domination and violence.

It is certainly possible to do some serious damage to the anal/rectal area even *without* violent anal penetration, and probably more so if the penis is large. Just ask any *MAN* who has been prison (and, of course, men can be and are raped outside of prison) raped, that is, experienced forcible anal rape, a common problem in prison. With modern medical treatment, death is not too likely, but it certainly would be possible to bleed out in some cases and or die later of a resulting infection, and it's certainly possible to permanently damage someone in that area.

Further, violent penetration of the vagina, let alone the anus, with or without a large penis can do serious damage as well. Again ladies, guys that ask this kind of question are why your parents worry for you...

Question: Can you get pregnant through anal sex?
Is your butt sore after anal sex?
Which is safer sex -- the anus or the vagina?
Can a woman get pregnant from anal sex?

THEY ASKED YOU WHAT?!

Answer: As we noted in the discussion on ways to get pregnant, anal sex is pretty unlikely to result in pregnancy, but it's not impossible. The anus is real close (duh!) to the vaginal opening. Semen that goes in the butt has to come back out some time. If some of the sperm make that short trip to the vagina and start swimming up where they are supposed to be, pregnancy can and has happened. You still need to use a condom.

As to the sore butt question, yes, hurried, inexperienced, anal sex can result in a very sore if not damaged butt. It's kind of like other forms of sex. If it hurts, you are doing it wrong, and you can be causing some real damage. If it hurts, *STOP*. At this point in life, it's better to avoid doing it at all. No honest person will describe anal sex, *especially unprotected anal sex,* as safer sex. Yes, you are not as likely to get pregnant, but it isn't safe in the sense young people desperately want it to be...

Question: If your a guy can u have sex with urself in the butt?

Answer: If you could, you guys would already be doing it, because young guys will put it in anything. Seriously, next time you have an erection, try to bend it around to your anus. Really, just try. Let us know how it worked... Let's see, poor text speak, shaky reasoning; yet another question that should make you fear that your generation's intellectual gene pool is seriously flawed...

Question: If a penis gets stuck in your butt hole, can you shit it out? (don't worry, I rephrased "shit" to "poop" when I read this in class)

Answer: While people who work in emergency rooms have endless stories about people who come in with various object stuck up their rectums (because, unlike the vagina, the rectum and lower intestines may not be endless, but stuff can go a looong way up there, far out of your reach), you must remember that the penis is attached to a human. While there are muscles in the anal sphincter that closes off the anus, there is not the large amount of muscular tissue to cramp up the way a vagina can, and it highly unlikely that the penis will get stuck such that the man could not remove it. Certainly the muscles that you use to poop will help push the penis out of the rectum, because that's what those muscles are for, pushing stuff out.

Question: Can you get sexually transmitted diseases through butt sex?

Answer: Oh yes indeed! The thin, easily damaged nature of anal/rectal tissue makes it ***much easier to transmit any and all Sexually Transmitted Diseases via anal sex! Again, any and all STDs can be transmitted more easily during unprotected anal sex.*** That is, HIV, herpes, chlamydia, syphilis, gonorrhea, HPV, and *all* the others. Even if you are careful and don't damage the delicate rectal tissue, it is thinner and germs find it much easier to move through it into the bloodstream. Again, vaginal tissue is relatively tough, and has some resistance to many germs even if it gets injured. Anal/rectal tissue does not have this resistance, especially if it is injured. As always, the transmission can go the other way to the penis and urethra on the male. A penis infection *is not* fun. Condoms are at least as important for anal sex as they are for vaginal sex.

SEXUALITY

I *could* call this the "Am I gay?" chapter because that question, directly asked or implied, comes up so often in this context. In fact, it encompasses all the vast variety of topics and obsessions of the newly sexual, including romantic, feelings, commitments, and attempts at seduction. Like all things to do with the emotional life of teenagers, it can range from the heartbreakingly sincere to jaw-dropping crassness.

Question: I once thought about sticking my finger in my butthole. Does this make me homosexual?

Answer: No, yes, possibly, whatever. While homosexuals have anal sex, wanting to touch and explore the anal area does not in and of itself make one gay, or even "bi-curious." It may just mean you are curious about those sensations and feelings. Many straight men and women find they enjoy anal stimulation. But, please wash your hands afterwards.

Question: I have a friend in our grade who has had sex 9 times... Is she a whore?

Is it bad to have already had sex 10 times with 3 different people at this age?

Answer: Well, first let's define our terms precisely. The technical definition of a whore the same as that for a prostitute, a woman who has sex for money. If your friend is getting paid, then she technically would be a whore or prostitute. In our culture, the term "whore" is often used to describe a girl or woman who has a lot of sex with different people even if she is not getting paid, and it is always a very derogatory term, and certainly not the way to talk about anyone you would consider to be a friend. It's also not exactly fair, because guys who have a lot of sex don't get called the same type of names.

So, overall, avoid calling people whores, the same way you would avoid using the "N" word. Just because a girl likes to have a lot of sex does not mean she is getting paid or that she is a bad person, though there is a lot of ancient cultural tradition that these things are both bad things in a woman. In the end, it just may mean she likes to have sex.

Now, I am definitely not saying it is good to have a lot of sex partners at your age. There is a lot of anecdotal and a growing body of scientific studies that show that girls who become sexually active at your age may have other negative things going on in their life, whether it is family issues or depression or combinations of these and other factors. There are some indications that early sexual activity can affect a girl's self-image for much of her life—or that a bad self-mage contributes to early sexual activity, it's hard to tell which. *Overall, girls and women who wait to start sex until they are some years older than 8th grade seem to be healthier in their personal life and outlook.* Intellectual and emotional maturity matters a lot, not just the fact that your body is grown enough to physically have sex. People your age don't always make good choices in critical issues like birth control and preventing STDs because your brain doesn't think about long term costs and consequences the way a more mature person does. The part of your brain that thinks about those things is one of the last things to mature in humans.

All of these things or none of them may apply to your friend. She may just be a very sexual person, and hopefully she's smart about it. But that's not something you can count on in a 14 year old, and the scientific data we have shows that, more often than not, it's unhealthy emotionally and physically. So first: be a friend, don't give her labels like "whore," and be there to support and help her if she does get in trouble. And of course, you have to make your own choices in life, and you certainly don't have to make hers.

Question: What does sex feel like?

Why does sex feel good?

Why is sex pleasurable if we are not suppose to do it?

Why do you only teach us about the bad things that come from sex, but we're never taught about the good that come from it? Do you expect us to learn it on our own?

Answer: Why? Sex feels good so we will do it a lot, have babies, and stay together to raise them! Sex is an evolutionary adaptation (or a gift from God, take your pick) that makes sure we will produce offspring and take care of them long enough so *they* can grow up, have sex, and make more babies. Really, would we spend so much time and effort on something so messy and incon-venient if it wasn't *really* important to us from an evolutionary and survival standpoint? So, historically, humans have had no trouble discovering the fun, pleasurable part of sex for just those reasons. It's built into us.

The survival/evolutionary point of sex is to exchange and mix up our genetic material, so that creatures have more chance for genetic mutations that will help us be more successful as creatures. Bacteria started doing this at least a couple billion years ago, and plants, animals, and fungi have been evolving various ways of doing so since. In humans, making it fun, exciting, and powerfully attractive has worked well (there are seven billion of us).

Now to the "not suppose to" part. That last, ***"Why do you only teach us about the bad things..."*** question is one of the best I've ever been asked, and I'm surprised some version of it hasn't been asked more often by other than the very smart, thoughtful young lady who penned it. Those warnings and protections have everything to do with what human cultures have learned over thousands of years. Humans are physically able to have sex and reproduce before they are old enough to understand the importance, consequences, emotional and physical costs, and risks of an activity that can change their life for the rest of their life. Why? Because teenagers, especially middle school age teenagers, are still mentally and emotionally children in many ways. As I discuss elsewhere, your brain will not finish growing up for several years after you can physically make a baby (insulting, I know, when you feel so grown up, but look around at your friends, you know it's true). Why did we evolve this somewhat messed up tendency? Because having babies was more important for species survival than being mature. Further, primitive ancestors had to grow up fast anyway, and they often had the responsibilities of an adult in their teens, ready or not. Another critical difference was that they also grew up surrounded by their tribal families constantly providing support as well as examples of adult behavior and how to raise babies from their earliest childhood. Our modern culture often does not provide the same training.

Historically, underage sex has also burdened societies with unwanted children that their underage biological parents cannot raise properly, and someone has to take care of those kids, or the culture then finds itself with messed-up adults who commit crimes, contribute poorly to society, and have more messed-up kids.

Think of it this way. Most people are physically big enough that they could probably operate a car when they 10 years old or so, but would you want to be on the road with a bunch of 4th or 5th graders at the wheel of the cars around you? Our cultural traditions and legal rules about drugs, alcohol, voting, and operating dangerous equipment all come from the same place. We realize that just because you can physically do something doesn't mean you should do it and it probably means you can't do it well or in a way that will not burden or endanger the rest of us. If you are honest with yourself, it's hard to deny this. How many of your friends are really ready for children, STDs, or any kind of mature relationship?

Question: Why do teenage boys have wet dreams?

Answer: The general medical consensus is that this just the boy's body trying out and exercising the sexual equipment. It almost certainly has to do with the fact that, as teenagers, with all the testosterone raging through our bodies, we are very sexually wound up, and are suddenly *very* aware of girls (or whoever...) and sexuality. It's hardly surprising that our dreams often give us vivid sexual experiences that lead to orgasm/ejaculation. Not everybody has wet dreams, and not all of our sexual dreams lead to ejaculation, and as is the case with many dreams, we don't always remember them when we awaken. You may or may not be having sex dreams yet, and you may never have one that goes to ejaculation, so don't worry about it.

Question: Why don't girls have wet dreams as guys have wet dreams?

Answer: They do! More accurately, they have sex dreams, sometimes to the point of orgasm, just like guys and for the same growing-up-fast-suddenly-aware-of-boys-and-sexuality reasons boys do. Now they are usually not "wet" because women don't usually have the same kind of ejaculation men do (though they can certainly awake to an aroused, "wet" vagina), but they can have sex dreams that are just as vivid as men and boys'. Now again, if this hasn't happened to you girls, don't panic. Dreams are very strange things, and not everyone even remembers the dreams they have, and hardly anyone has sex dreams all the time.

Question: What is the best way to seduce a girl? How do you turn a girl on?

Answer: Sorry, that sort of "how to?" is not part of the curriculum in Family Life—like anyone has the whole seduction thing figured out anyway. But look, you are probably starting to figure out that women are really, *really* complex creatures. That's part of the fun. There is no one rule or set of rules for getting along with them. It can seem that they only like the bad, gangsta dudes, because many girls go through a phase of liking the "bad boys" to some extent, and you are feeling the same frustration girls feel when it seems guys only like the "sluts." Sure, being handsome and studly helps. Being a successful athlete helps. Being rich helps, but none of these things are guarantees, because there are lots of men who are none of these things who do great with women.

A good place to start is to read the *Twilight* books, and/or see the movies (but that's a poor second choice to the reading, like most movies made from books). Now, these books have been rightly criticized for a somewhat sexist portrayal of Bella as a helpless female in an old fashion relationship with a guy.

So what. It also an over-simplification of a scenario that still pushes the romantic buttons of *many* girls and women, and it pushes them hard. That is why these stories are so insanely popular. What do you have in these stories? Two intelligent, thoughtful (okay ridiculously good looking) guys who focus entirely on protecting and making happy the girl they love. They listen to her, try to understand her, and don't totally focus on having sex with her, though that possibility makes them crazy as it does all young men. As a result of this attention, Bella very much would like to have sex with either of the guys, but particularly the thoughtful, soulful Edward. Of course, none of those things affect everyone, or every girl the same way, and a lot of girls just think the books and Bella are dumb.

So hear me out. The approach you see in the *Twilight* books works in the long run and works more often with more women than anything else. ***Be considerate and thoughtful and kind. Yes, be nice!*** Shocking, I know. It doesn't work all the time with all girls, because a lot of them can be kind of masochistic at your age, but it works more than anything else. Actually listen to what they say and try to understand it, even if it makes your eyes glaze over and drives you nuts. The things they say are important, and it can be the best way to learn what makes girls tick, though you will find what they say is important can change moment by moment. Try to have a sense of humor. If there is one universal thing women say they want in a man, after consideration and thoughtfulness, it's humor. Now humor can be a mine field, and some of my most deeply embarrassing, cold sweat inducing memories are of failed attempts at humor or coolness for the benefit of girls, but go for it. The mistakes you make now will make you a better guy later when it really counts. This doesn't mean you have to stop being a guy and enjoying all the heroic, insane, skateboard-off-a-cliff-with-a-bottle-rocket-in-your-nose things we do in sports and just being young guys. Girls like heroes too, but real ones like policemen, firemen and military guys, not just the suicidal dumb ones.

So, thoughtfulness, consideration, and respect will get you farther than anything else. It's also a pretty good way to approach life in general, sort of the golden rule thing.

And in the end, a lot of it is hormones and pheromones and you may never have a clue why someone adores you or ignores you. But the fun IS in the chase......

Question: Why is sex short? (clearly written in a girl's hand writing)
How long does an average male last when they have sex?
Ho do you build stamina? (the last two clearly from concerned boys)

Answer: A universal question (and endless source of humor), especially from young women having their first sexual experiences. Mostly sexual encounters at this age are short because young men and boys are sexually wound up, in a hurry, and inexperienced. That's just the way it is for guys when they first have sex. They are so keyed up sexually that they have an ejaculation/orgasm very quickly, sometimes within seconds of starting intercourse, sometimes even before starting intercourse. By nature, they lose interest in the subject almost immediately thereafter ejaculation. Because young couples lack privacy, they are often nervous and stressed and that stress also makes for quick sexual encounters.

Due to inexperience, and the natural, innocently clueless selfishness of sexually self-obsessed young guys, they most often don't (or in fairness, can't) spend the time before intercourse on the girl's needs. Due to the same inexperience, girls usually don't understand their own needs, and even if they have a clue, they are often very shy and reluctant to explain or ask for what they need to make sex good for them because in their mind that makes them admit they "want it" and therefore they must be bad and slutty. So, it's hardly surprising that while guys find almost any sexual experience great, many girls find their early sexual encounters too short, sometimes physically or emotionally painful, and bewildering ("What's all the fuss about sex anyway?" is a common feeling), boy-centered, and not at all the romantic, sensual, life changing experience they hoped for.

Patience, self-awareness, and the willingness to make sure that the girl is getting what she needs from the sexual experience mean a lot. Stamina comes with time, experience, and putting the girl/woman first.

Question: How do lesbians have sex?
Can lesbians have sex?
What do gay guys do and what do lesbians do together?
How do men have sex?

Answer: Gay men have oral, manual and anal sex. Not all that different from straight sex, except for the use of the anus instead of a vagina.

Lesbian women have of oral, manual, and other ways of rubbing various parts, particularly the clitoris, together. Not really all that different from straight sex except for the lack of a penis, which, if you have been paying attention, isn't necessarily required for a woman's sexual enjoyment.

Question: Why are girls more nastyer in bed then guys?

Answer: Are they now? By nastier, I take it that you mean the girls you have been in bed with are more enthusiastic and adventurous about sex than the boys you have been in bed with? Are they more aggressive, enthusiastic, and adventurous about sex than you think girls should be? Is this a bad or a good thing? Everyone is different, and what's "nasty" for some is just part of good clean sex for others. "Nasty" in the sense of sexual enjoyment and enthusiasm is generally considered a good thing, as long as it doesn't also mean that foolish or dangerous risks are being taken. Labels can be tricky.

Question: Why don't girls want sex?

Answer: Ahhh... The flip side of the question above. It's not so much that they don't want it (they do), it's that many guys want it *all the time*, while girls and women are both more selective about who they have sex with, and, as we have discussed, their desire for sex is more dependent on their monthly cycle. Further, as we have also discussed, sex carries a lot more weight with women because it simply can have a much higher cost. You simply have to remember that, evolutionarily, women are designed to get pregnant. That is the bottom line, biological/evolutionary purpose of their bodies. They can enjoy sex as much or more than guys, but whether they have birth control or not, that potential is always out there, and pregnancy exacts a huge cost on their body and their life, for the rest of their life. However much a girl likes sex, it will never be the same thing for her as it is for a guy, who can have intercourse, be done and say "whoopee, let's do it again!" with one partner or another. His evolutionary job is to spread as much of his semen (that is, his genes) around as he can, though he also has the conflicting role and desire to help raise and provide for at least some of his offspring.

A woman, whether she actually thinks about it or not, is almost instinctively judging whether this guy she is going to have sex with has good genes to produce a healthy offspring, and whether he will be around to raise any offspring. She may not in fact care about these things with any particular guy, but it is part of what the emotional and intellectual conversation her body has with her.

So, you can't ever expect that on average, women will want sex the way guys do. They may want it as much or more *sometimes*, but *not all the time*, for very sound emotional and evolutionary reasons.

Question: Why do us men look at girl's breasts?

Answer: Humans, as a species, have some of the best eyesight in nature. Maybe not as precise at a distance as a hawk's, not as good at night as a cat's, but all around better than almost anything out there. Men are more visually oriented than women, on average, and visual cues play an important part in signaling sexual maturity and availability for both sexes. Pubic hair is one cue that a person is physically mature and ready for sex. Tallness, broad shoulders, and beards signal a man's maturity. A waistline, curvy hips, and buttocks and breasts are the visual signals in women. Breast tissue itself is mostly fat, and is not needed for nursing a baby. Entirely flat-chested women nurse with no problems and you may have noticed that monkeys, apes, and most animals don't have anything like human breasts as far as size. So large, or at least larger, breasts probably evolved to visually signal us as creatures that stand upright and face each other that a woman is mature and available for mating and raising a child. Some evolutionary biologists propose that full breasts present the same kind of visual image from in front as female buttocks do from behind, and a mature girl or woman's hips and buttocks are a pretty universal sexual image even in cultures where big breasts are not that big a deal. Whatever the reason, early human women who had noticeably larger breasts mated more often and had more babies than those who did not, so that the larger breast genes got passed on more often than not. Even small-breasted human women have bigger breasts than virtually all animals, so that visual cue seems to be enough, because most women don't have huge breasts, yet they do very well attracting and keeping mates. (9, 10, 11)

Question: Can tranny's that turn into guys have huge dicks and do they have boners?

Answer: I'm sure the *transsexual* ("tranny" can be a very offensive term to transsexual people) person making the change from female to male has some say on the size of the penis they are to be fitted with. Remember, this person starts as a female, and may not feel the need for the "huge dick" that you as a male assumes he would want. There are also limitations to what the surgery can accomplish. For female to male transsexuals, one of the surgical options is a *"phalloplasty" where* the erection is caused by an actual inflatable insert to the artificially created penis, so erections themselves are no problem. Another option is a *"metoidioplasty"* where a "penis" is constructed from the labia tissue and the clitoris.

Question: What is a girl to say when a guy says he loves her and he thinks it's time to have sex? What if they're really close friends? but she isn't ready.
and....
What if you liked a guy a lot and he's had sex but you haven't and he asked if you wanted to have sex with him and

you consider it but you don't know if
your ready then what do you do?

Answer: I love these questions for several reasons. First, they are universal. Every young woman and most young couples are faced with this "first time" decision at some point. Guys think about this decision too, more than many might assume. But for girls, this is a big one. Second, it goes to the issue of self-knowledge and realizing that you do in fact know what is the right thing to do, but that doing the right thing can be tough. You already answered the question when you said "you don't know if you're ready" and "but she isn't ready." That's the answer right there. If you know yourself well enough to realize you are not ready, You should be able to say so, and that should be the end of the discussion at this point in your relationship.

Now, I realize it's not that easy. The "no" can break up a relationship that is otherwise wonderful and special. Unfortunately, we live in a time when many guys grow up assuming that girls owe them sex and they will sometimes move on or seek it from someone else if they don't get it. **Girls don't owe guys anything sexually other than honesty and consideration.** While most guys do try to be really decent and want to respect and accept the girl's decision, that sexual imperative is hard for guys to ignore, especially when everything they see around them tells them they "should" be having sex because "everyone" is. The fact is, you may be surprised how understanding a guy can be about these things. Or not.

I also realize many girls experience the feeling that they "just want to get it over with" and have sex once to be done with the big issue for a while, even if they don't have sex for a long time afterwards until they find someone special. While that feeling is understandable, I'm pretty sure that's not a good enough reason to expose yourself to all the emotional and physical issues that go with sex just to "get it over with." Losing your virginity is by definition a special, once in a lifetime experience. It would be nice to experience it with someone who you care about and who cares about you.

You have to take a long view on this, which is *really* hard at your age. At some point you are going to have sex. ***It does not have to be now, and, for all sorts of good reasons, shouldn't be now.*** You are all going to have boyfriends and girlfriends and lovers and possibly husbands and wives at some point. It is almost never going to be the person you are with now. If you are right for each other, you will get past this. If not there *will* be other special people in your life.

Question: If you've had sex already how should you approach your parents about it?

Answer: Good, at least you are thinking that it would be good to talk about it, and that means you have a good enough relationship with your parents to consider the discussion. Not knowing your parents, it's hard to say just how to begin. Start with whichever one you can have heart-to-heart talks with most easily. It can be tough for daughters to talk with their dads about this just because it's dad's nature to be protective of (and not always reasonable about) daughters, and many, but by no means all, people find this easier to approach with Mom. I know my wife was much more practical and matter-of-fact about this than I was, however cool I wanted to be about the subject. Sons can usually do all right with either Mom or Dad.

It also depends on *your* attitude. My older daughter was very mature and careful, and went to Planned Parenthood at 16 or so when she decided she was going to have sex, got birth control, condoms and everything, completely independently and without a word to her parents. So we had educated her properly, and

she took good care of herself, however much we would have preferred that she discuss it with one of us before jumping in. But she
NEVER told us anything about her sex life, and flatly denied having any for years, even when things like used condoms showed
up in her bedroom trashcan. Any attempt on her parents' part to
discuss it was met by plugged ears and chanted "na-na-na, I don't
want to talk about it." My younger daughter, on the other hand,
would have long talks with my wife (Dad's don't get in on this I
find, to their infinite relief) discussing the most intimate details of
her love life, birth control options, and what to expect from boys
and lovers.

There is an old standby piece of advice that works well when
you are to the point of discussing the subject; you saw it described
in the Family Life video we showed you in sixth grade. The idea is
to bring it up while driving in the car with whichever parent you
choose to talk to, but not both. Mom or Dad has to keep their eyes
on the road, so you don't have that scary eye contact thing, and
they can't just freak out, because they are driving. Not that they
will freak out, but it is a more controlled situation.

However you approach it, just lay out in a calm manner what
happened. If you were smart enough to use birth control and protection (notice that they are not the same thing, *you need both*),
make sure you tell them that too. If you didn't, you are probably
going to get an earful, but at least you will get help and advice
on what to do next. Most parents wisely schedule a visit to the
gynecologist immediately for their daughters in this situation,
and hopefully you have been seeing one at least once a year since
you started your period, if you are a girl and have begun having
periods.

Your parents may not be happy with you, but you will almost
certainly be surprised by how understanding they are. They will be
hugely relieved that you came to them about it, and flattered that
you felt you could. They had the same first time sexual experience

at some point in their life, and for them it was not as long ago as you would think. In the end, they want to make sure you are not harmed physically or emotionally, though they know that love and sex will certainly give you some emotional hard knocks at some point. That's life. One of the things nearly everyone realizes at some point in their life is that however crazy you think your parents are, they really are doing what they think is best out of love for you. It may be hard to see now, but at some point it will be obvious that they were trying to do what's right, and sometimes you need to just go with that.

Question: Could a gay couple have sex up the penis hole?

Answer: Okay dude, seriously. Next time you are handling your penis—and I know you do—look at the penis. Then look at the hole on the end of your penis. Look at the penis again, especially if it has an erection. Look at the hole on the end of the penis again. Is a penis *ever* going to fit in there? Or again, as we have discussed on other occasions when questions about putting penises in inappropriately small orifices have been asked, if your penis somehow could fit it there, wouldn't that just be *really* embarrassing for the owner of the penis??

Note to reader: I truly don't know where some of these questions come from. As a teacher, you try not to ridicule and humiliate the person asking some of these questions, but sometimes it's either that or being reduced to praying for the future of the human species and despair about the quality of the intellectual gene pool that is being loosed upon the world. There *are* sexual practices where people put objects up the urethra. So, whatever.... To me, reading between the lines of this question, this person is hoping that there is some other way for gay men to have intercourse other than oral or anal sex, because he can't deal with the prospect of those acts.

Question: Did caveman have sex?

Answer: I assume you mean did cave men and women have sex? Though, no doubt there were gay cavemen. Of course, that's where baby cave people came from, and eventually all the rest of us too.

Question: Do you think my mom lost her verginaty?

Answer: *(poor thing, so sad to destroy illusions...)* Well, if we define virginity traditionally as a person who has not had penis-in-vagina sex, which, in turn, is how virtually every mother gets pregnant, then it's highly unlikely that your mom retained her virginity. Now, if she had artificial insemination at a doctor's office, and had never had sex otherwise, you could argue the point.

Question: How does a guy that has turned his penis into a vagina go number one?

Answer: All transsexual transformations begin with a lot of counseling to make sure the person really knows what they want and is clear on what they will have to do. Months and sometimes years of female hormone treatments follow to reduce the male sex characteristics and bring out the female characteristics like less body/ facial hair, wider hips and so on. During a typical male to female sex change operation, it is common practice to invert the skin of the penis inside of the person's body and suture (sew) it there to form an artificial but sexually functional vagina that can be used for intercourse. That's an oversimple description of a complex bit of plastic surgery, but that's basically what happens. During the sex change surgery, the urethra is re-routed and sutured into a location at the top of the artificial vagina where the urethra exits in a woman so that the person urinates the same way people born as women do.

Question: Would they turn a vagina right side out for a girl to get a penis?

Answer: No. You are asking about the reverse of the above operation. The switch from female to male is more surgically complicated than male to female. It also starts with hormone treatments that cause a beard to grow and bring out the other desired male characteristics like more defined muscles and a deeper voice. One option, as noted previously, is a surgery to construct a "penis" from the clitoris and labia tissue. The other surgical option is to create a pocket in the external tissue for an insertable/removable, inflatable artificial penis implant to simulate erections. An artificial scrotum is often created from the vulva's labia majora (the larger lips on the outside of the vulva). All this follows surgery to remove the uterus, fallopian tubes and ovaries, as well as breast reduction surgery.

Question: What's a MILF?

Answer: It is a slang acronym for *M*other *I*'d *L*ike to Have Sex With (you can figure out the *"F"* part). Before you use it, consider whether you would want your friends or people you know referring to your mom that way. The term simply refers to sexually attractive women who have children, like it's a shock that someone could be a mom and still be hot. Keep in mind that your dad probably still thinks of your mom that way.

Question: What if your having a thing with a 19 yr. old & U just made out? What would that be?

Answer: For the 19 year old, it's verging on serious legal trouble. It is illegal in California for someone over 18 to have sex with someone under 18. If it happens, it's called "statutory rape," which means even if the younger person voluntarily and happily had sex with the older person, under the law it's just like forcible rape because the under- age person is not considered to be mature enough to make that decision for themselves and understand what they are getting into. It is part of how our society protects young people from being sexually exploited. That legal age varies from state to state, but nowhere in the U.S. is it less than 16.

Now, according to your question, there has been no actual sex in the relationship, so technically, it is still legal. However, the fact is, no 19 year old is going to be in a relationship like the one you describe without sex becoming part of the relationship, and if you are honest with yourself, you know that is true. And, you have to ask, why is a 19 year old having a relationship with a 14 year old rather than someone closer to their age? There are a lot of legal minefields here for the older person, and a lot of emotional, physical, and social risks for the young person. It's not a healthy situation, and everyone involved is not being honest with themselves, and especially dishonest with the younger person.

Just to put a cap on this, keep in mind an important statistic that doesn't get as widespread notice as it should. In the U.S., over 70% of teenage pregnancies are actually caused by males 20 and over, NOT by teenage males. Further, males age 20 or more cause FIVE TIMES as many births among middle school age girls compared to births in the same age group caused middle school age boys. It's pretty basic biology. Young girls like older boys, and they are *very* vulnerable to manipulation by an older non-teen willing to take the legal risks of seducing under-age girls. (34)

Question: (don't read aloud in school) I've been bi (bisexual) for about a year now and I'm very curious about it as well. My sister is as well, and she's told mom but I'm not comfortable telling her. Should I? Please note, the "don't read in school" part was on the actual question slip and I didn't.

Answer: I'm assuming from the handwriting and the tone of the question that this is a guy, though the answer would be the same if it is a girl. The difference would be that bisexuality and homosexuality in girls and women are generally (but by no means always) easier for our parents and society to accept than they are in boys and men. That just seems to be the way it is nowadays.

Not knowing the person asking the question or their family makes it harder for me to give advice. Certainly the fact that your sister has discussed this with Mom, and that Mom appears to be accepting of her sexual situation, would indicate to me that she would be accepting of you as well. She may not be happy with either of you and your sexuality, but accepting is worth a lot. You know yourself, and you know Mom. Maybe your sister could be there to help the conversation along, because it sounds like you have a good relationship with her too. In the long term, talking it out is usually better than not, even if it can be tough to start the conversation.

Question: I caught my parents having sex one time and I didn't know what to do or say. What should I have done?

Answer: You'd probably be amazed how many people that's happened to. It's embarrassing to walk in on anyone who is having sex. It's worse when it's your parents because everyone knows they don't have sex, except to make you, and that thought is gross enough for most people. There's not much to say other than "sorry, excuse me," and then leave the room immediately. Some day you will look back at the incident and laugh about it.

It wasn't always this way. For most of human history (and still in many parts of the world today) families lived in single room homes where everyone (Mom, Dad, sisters and brothers, and probably a grandparent or two as well) slept in one room, often in the same bed or, more likely, on the floor. People still had sex, right there in the middle of all the other warm bodies, and our modern idea of privacy would be considered pretty exotic and an unimaginable luxury. Children may have not actively watched their parents have sex in those times, but they were plenty aware of it, and between that and watching the farm animals, they learned most of what people thought they needed to know about the subject.

As to you and your interrupted parents, all you can do is excuse yourself, say you're sorry, and move on. You were embarrassed, but no one was hurt, and in the end, it's just no big deal. Be glad your parents still dig each other enough to have sex. Not everybody's do. You might, however, remember to knock next time, or make enough noise entering the house that people know you are there before your trip over each other.

Questions: Why do guys like other men?
Is it true people that are not like other people are born that way?
Why do gay guys talk like girls?
I can't tell if I'm a boy or a girl. I'm so confused....

Answer: The issue of sexuality seems to be huge these days. We live in such a sexualized age that declaring what you are, and discussing the sexuality of others, is a major conversation topic, especially at your age. It wasn't always so. For much of America's history, you grew up who you were, kept quiet about any part of yourself you thought was "depraved" whether straight or gay, and lived whatever sexual life you had. Those things were private. And for the most part, people minded their own business and didn't ask or care who you had sex with as long as you kept it private.

Now, I realize people have a lot of religious, moral, and personal opinions on sexuality. I'm going to give you the best current scientific information I have. You have to make the religious/moral decisions yourself based on your own beliefs.

You are probably getting tired of hearing me say it, but people are both different and the same at the same time. There is a huge range of sexual preferences. Some people are totally straight (meaning they only want to have sex with the opposite sex), and the idea of having sex with a member of the same sex is just not going to work for them. They can find nothing attractive or erotic about touching other people in the same places they already have.

Some people are totally gay or homosexual. They find members of their own sex to be totally hot and sexually attractive, while the opposite sex holds little interest for them, though unlike most straight people, most gay people have had some straight sex. They are perfectly happy this way, and enjoy their lives as such.

There are some transsexual who feel strongly, "that they were born in the wrong body." That is, all their life they have felt that they should be the sex they are not, and want desperately to make the change to the opposite sex's body if they can. These are often the people who seek to have the sex change operations you have asked about. Other transsexual people are perfectly happy with the sex/gender body they have, choosing to live their lives as the sex they were born in, or by dressing and living as the opposite sex. Many like their own sex, the opposite gender or both.

There has been an increasing amount of scientific study of the differences in straight and gay people over recent decades, and some consistent findings are emerging. We now know that there are all manner of gay animals: giraffes, sea gulls, penguins, dolphins (who appear to have sex for fun with everyone they know), and pretty much any type of animal that's been studied enough for us to notice these things turns out to have gay members of the species. Now animals don't "choose" a gay life style. They just do what comes naturally without thought or worry or about what others think, and they have no religion to guide or judge them. So, these things are out there in the wild, and it's hard to argue they are not "natural." At least the animals don't care whether we care or not.

We now know that there are subtle but definite differences in the brains of men and women. Without going into all those structural differences here, studies of the brains of gay and straight people have shown the gay men have brains with a structure more like that of women, and lesbian women have brains that are structured more like men. That would seem to explain why gay men often (but by no means always) act and talk in a feminine way, while some gay women can seem very masculine.

There appears to be a genetic part in this. Studies of identical twins (who are genetically the same) separated at birth show that if one grows up to be homosexual, the other twin is highly likely to be gay as well even though they weren't raised together.

Genetics are not the only factor, however. You will remember when we discussed how the male and female anatomy developed while you were tiny fetuses inside your mom, and that we said the hormones released during development controlled much of that sex organ growth. Well, those hormones also direct how the brain grows and is structured, that is, whether it becomes more like a male or female brain. It is thought, though experiments to prove this would be tough to carry out, that if these hormones are not sequenced in the "normal" way, or if something disrupts or changes what hormones (because both male and female hormones are important at different times to the growth of both sexes in the uterus) get released at critical points in the brain development, that the structure of the brain could be pushed toward more that of the opposite sex, perhaps setting the person up to be gay. Genetic tendencies almost certainly influence this as well, but these hormonal shifts can occur independently of genetic action. Independent of genetics, there are studies that show that the youngest son of several sons has an increased statistical chance of being gay. No one is sure why, but it may be due to how the mom's body handles the hormonal development of a male fetus after several male children.

It should be emphasized that these differences are subtle and not obvious. They become apparent in statistical studies of a number of people. But, like everything else about people, the individual variations can be great without meaning anything definite. You can't take a brain scan of some sort and clearly say, "This person is straight," or, "This person is gay." What we can say is that if you study a lot of brains of straight and gay people, the statistics show a numerical matchup or trend between the physical characteristics of various brain structures and "maleness" or "femaleness."

These issues aside, it also appears true that while men are certainly straight, gay or bisexual, women by nature (that is, aside from upbringing and cultural influences) have a more open sexual nature, and that it is generally easier for them to have sexual attractions and relations with either sex. Studies across many cultures, sexually liberal and conservative, seem to indicate this is true. So, even though it is cool and trendy for some young women to declare their bisexuality these days, it also appears to be a real aspect of at least a significant portion of the female population. Certainly some of this is cultural too. It is simply easier in American culture for a woman to be openly bisexual than it is for a man.(23)

And no, you can't always tell by looking, and most people's "gaydar" is hit or miss at best. Very straight men in prison have gay sex, because they tend to be young, sexual men, and gay sex is the only sex available to them. Once they are out of prison, most never have gay sex again. It may shock you, but gay pro athletes make up as large, if not larger by some estimates, a part of the athlete population as gay people do in the rest of the population. Now certainly, many gay people make no effort to hide their gayness, but don't count on being able to tell just by looking.

Being humans, with strong social and cultural influences in our lives, much of what we actually do comes from the culture we live in. Cultures like the ancient Greeks and Romans didn't much care who you had sex with, and people of both sexes had sex with whoever they wanted. The classical Greeks in particular thought true love and understanding, both sexual and emotional, existed primarily in homosexual relationships, and that straight sex was mainly for fun and procreation. Most human cultures are more conservative, feeling sex is properly for keeping men and women together in families.

So, it appears that people are mostly "born that way," straight or gay or, "whoopee, it's all fun." By the time people are in their teens, they start to realize who they are attracted to, and whether they are straight or gay or not. They may be not sure, and it may be they are truly bisexual and like both. But, if you are honest with yourself, you know, or will know soon, who you are.

However, we are also humans, the creature that has the brain and awareness to make choices about any aspect of our lives. We can be whatever we want or think we should be. But, asking a gay person to live their life as a straight person is just as hard for them (though it may make it easier to get along in society) as asking a straight person to live their life gay. It doesn't work, and it sets people up to live unhappy lives. One of the main themes of this book is avoiding self-deception and being honest with yourself. You are already aware of your sexuality, or you soon will be. Let that be who you are, and accept that sexuality, be happy with it, and accept what other people are as well. I try not to preach too much on this topic, but love and happiness are always in short supply. Take it where you find and it, and let others do the same. If your beliefs make that hard for you, and I don't discount how important that can be in a person's life, at least try to live and let live. (24)

Question: If I have gotten sexual urges in class. How do I make them go away?
How do I stop having sexual fantasies about.... (insert a boy or girl's name, there are questions like this every year, and they can be boy-girl, girl-boy, boy-boy and girl-girl. Often there is an air of real distress because the person writing the question is shocked to find they have erotic feeling for someone of the same sex.)

Answer: This happens to everyone, and not only teenagers. Look, there are lots of impulses we have day to day that we can't immediately act on because of the circumstances: we *don't* start a food fight in a movie theater, we *don't* go to the bathroom anywhere we want to, we *don't* yell "fire!" in a crowded room. You just don't do it, and you deal with the impulses that make you think about trying it. It's part of becoming a mature human. Sexual impulses and urges are the same, however powerful they are. Get your mind back on your school work, the lecture, the test coming up, and move on. It will pass, but there is no magic technique to make this basic part of our being and imaginations go away. Having fantasies about someone you like and are attracted to is also part of the game. It's part of being human, and as distracting at they are, get used to it; you will be having them the rest of your life, whether you're a boy/man or girl/woman, straight or gay. It means you're alive. Enjoy it.

Question: So like when one gets horny; why like I really can't understand?

Answer: "Getting horny" is simply a slang term for being seriously in the mood for sex. That is, feeling that you want and "need" sex. It's a combination of physical and mental responses. Remember, no matter what you have learned about sexual anatomy, *the main sex organ is the human brain.* That's where it all starts and stops. As you should be realizing by now, this is a hugely complicated subject. All the things that affect every other part of a person's physical and mental being go into how much they desire sex. This includes their basic genetic makeup, health, upbringing, relationships, diet, physical condition, hormonal state, age, how long it's been since they had sex or masturbated, and so on...

Question: At what age should adults stop having sex?

Answer: If they are in good enough health, almost never. As people live longer and healthier lives, our ability to have sex has lasted longer too. People who exercise, eat healthy diets, and keep mentally active find that their desire and enjoyment of sex continues late into life. Usually their sexual activity is not at the same level as it was in their 20's or 30's, but can continue to be a great part of life. Now, you have heard of drugs like Viagara[tm] and others that help older men have erections. These work very well, but many, if not most, men don't need them (though the ads may make it seem that all older men need them) if their heart and circulatory systems are working well.

After menopause, when women stop having periods and producing eggs cells, many women find that the change in their hormones can reduce desire for sex and/or make it difficult because their vagina doesn't lubricate itself for sex as easily, even if they want sex. But increasingly, women who remain healthy and active enjoy sex as much or more (not having a period means there's several extra days for sex each month) than when they were younger, and the large variety of sexual lubricants available nowadays make sex just as easy and enjoyable as ever.

Just to illustrate this point, health workers are finding they have to re-educate seniors in many retirement communities about STDs and condoms because there are so many people having unprotected sex (after all, no one's getting pregnant at Leisure World) that they forget that they can get and transmit STDs at any age. The fastest growing STD population in many areas is the senior population!

Question: Do you have to be naked to have sex? Why do girls dress up in lingerai to have sex?

Answer: Well, neither option is required. To have sex, all you have to do is to get the sex organs together, and most clothing we wear nowadays has any number of options in that area that do not require complete undressing. Nakedness is fun, because we as a culture *do* dress, so undressing is automatically making ourselves vulnerable and available to the other person for sex, and we as a rule like the visual stimulation of naked bodies.

As to lingerie (l-i-n-g-e-r-i-e), it all plays to visual element in sexual arousal. Lingerie exposes or emphasizes the sexual parts of a woman's anatomy (breasts, hips, buttocks, vulva), or minimally and artfully hides them, while exposing the rest of the body. Either way, it is visually signaling "here it is, come and get it, and don't I look hot?"

But keep in mind that neither is required for sexual activity or enjoyment. People happily have sex all over the world without nakedness or lingerie, and have for thousands of years.

Question: How much does a hooker coast? (standard sex)

Answer: First, I of course have to remind you that prostitution is illegal, hooker being an old slang term for a prostitute. Even as a minor (under the age of 18) you can get in serious legal trouble if you are caught using a prostitute, or caught in a police sting operation soliciting for prostitution. Prostitution is only legal in the state of Nevada, outside of the Las Vegas city limits. Picking up and making use of a street prostitute is not only illegal, it's as dangerous as using street drugs, *because you never really know what you are getting, or in this case, catching.* Many of these women are serious and long time drug addicts who take poor or no care of their health, and they may have any or all the common STDs. On the other hand, high end professional call girls and escorts, or the prostitutes in the brothels in Nevada have much better safer sex practices and sexual health care than many non-prostitutes. How do you tell???

Prices range from a few dollars for a street prostitute in need of a drug fix, to $5000 to $10,000 dollars for a night with a top line call girl. Prices at the licensed, legal, and medically inspected houses of prostitution in Nevada start at few hundred dollars an hour for straight sex—and you still have to be legal age, 16 years old, in that state.

Question: I like a girl and I want to have sex with her but her brother will beat me up. What should I do?

Answer: Good for brother. Find another girl. I assume you have some indication that the girl is willing to have sex with you. If not, then you are really hopeless, and this is just another fantasy. Brothers are often protective, especially of little sisters, and it's hard to argue in this case. You don't deserve to be beaten up, but I wouldn't mess with the situation and just move on.

ALL THE OTHER STRANGE, FREAKY, AND SOMETIMES SAD STUFF THEY ASK ABOUT

Question: Is it possible for a man (??!!) to have both a penis and a vagina?

Answer: There is an almost infinite range of genetic and hormonal mix-ups and mash-ups that can happen during conception and gestation (pregnancy) resulting in a wide variety of human sexual anatomy. There *are* people with people with fully functional sets of both organs, that is, penis and testes along with vagina, uterus and ovaries. It is *extremely* rare, estimated at less than one in one hundred million births. Theoretically, such a person could impregnate themselves, but it would be genetically unadvisable, and it is physically unlikely that the person's erect penis could be bent into their own vagina. Any other combination that the fertile imagination of a 14-year-old can conjure has almost certainly occurred at some time, somewhere. Except in the very rare cases discussed above, the person usually does not really have both sets of organs, but mostly one kind or the other, with the second set of sex organs being smallish and under-developed. That is, what looks to be a small penis is just a large clitoris, and so on. The fact is, these anatomical mix-ups are considered to be very rare. This condition is called "intersex" and depending on how it's defined, can be very rare, or more common than many suspect.

> **Question:** Is animal sex legal/normal?
> Can a man make love to a dog?
> Can someone have sex with a horse?
> What is a donkey show?
> Has a horse had sex with a girl or a guy is it possible?

Answer: I assume you mean is it legal/normal *for humans to have sex with animals?* Animal sex itself is normal and legal for animals, and they wouldn't care if we make it illegal anyway. Humans having sex with animals is illegal throughout the United States as far as I know, and at best indicates very poor judgment on the part of any animal that would let itself be used this way. Further, it could be dangerous for the human, because most animals, especially dogs and horses, do in fact have better taste and judgment than to have sex with a human, and are not shy about making their feelings clear. As to whether it is normal or not, bestiality – the formal term for having sex with animals – certainly happens, but very few would call it normal. It just means, as noted previously, young guys (and occasionally some women) will have sex with *anything.*

A donkey show is a legendary nightclub show, traditionally said to be available in Tijuana, Mexico, where a woman has sex with a donkey. This proves also, if there was any doubt, that young men, especially young Navy and Marine recruits from Camp Pendleton and San Diego, will not only have sex with anything, they will *pay* to watch anything or anyone have sex with anything or anyone.

Again, for those of you who failed 7th grade life science and genetics, you cannot have a hybrid of a human and any other animal: horse, dog, cat and so on.

Question: Does James Bond have a disease? He's gotta have something.

Answer: *(Love this question!)* Who knows? At your age, I read all of the James Bond books a couple times, saw all the movies, and there was no mention of STDs. It *was* the 60's, however, and people paid less attention to those issues at that time. So, if you mean that he must have an STD because he appears to have so much unprotected sex, perhaps, but it wasn't exactly the point of the stories.

Question: Can conjoined twins be joined at the penis?

Answer: Yes, it's happened. Google it. Theoretically, it is possible for conjoined twins to be joined at any part of the body.

Question: How do elephants have sex?

Answer: They do it "doggy style!" Obviously, it is a somewhat ponderous affair, but they do it like any other four-legged animal.

Question: How badly can a man hurt a woman with his penis during sex? Could a huge black man kill a little Asian girl during sexual intercourse?
Is there a penis so big that it can brake all the organs inside a girl and kill her?

Can you kill a girl by eating her too rough?

Answer: Okay, some of you guys are seriously messed up. I mean it, you need some counseling. At best, you need to stop taking the hardcore porn you are seeing on line as any kind of example of how real people have sex.

The perennial sex, violence, and penis size guy question... Look, assuming you are referring to adult people having sex voluntarily, it's not a big deal. Again, the vagina can pass a baby, so the penis is just not that big. A large, long penis banging against the cervix at the top of the vagina is painful for most women, and people learn to avoid that if they are having sex where that is an issue. Some women, some of the time, like to experiment with vigorous, rough sex, just like we all have varying tastes in food and other things that are a matter of personal preference. This does not mean most women want anything to do with this type of activity all of the time. Further, if you are talking rape and violent, non-voluntary penetration, then it is possible to do real and conceivably fatal damage in this area.

Because of people like the one (*what am I saying? The "people" are guys!*) writing this question, there is a whole segment of the porn industry dedicated to enthusiastically demonstrating that it is possible for large black men to have sex with small women, Asian or otherwise. So what? And seriously, are only black men "large" and only Asian women "small?" How many girls out there want to have sex with a guy that wants to kill you with his penis, or have oral sex with you to death? Of course, a person asking this kind of question may not care whether a woman "wants" to have sex with them.

These questions remind us that there is always a certain proportion of boys/men for whom sex is about domination, humiliation, and violence, and not anything you could call "making love." It is probably part of most male's testosterone driven sexual makeup, and like most of our bad impulses, it is usually controlled. One only has to look at the repeated horrors of mass rape and violence against women during war down through the centuries to the present day, acts committed by otherwise decent, normal young men temporarily freed of inhibitions by the bloodlust of war, to know this is out there. This is why all cultures have intuitively sought to protect women from this part of our male nature.

Question: What is kinky sex?

Answer: The term "kinky sex" refers to any sexual acts or practices that someone else has defined as exotic or not normal. For some people it's virtually anything that's not man on top/ woman on the bottom, face to face, "missionary" sex. For other people, one person's "kinky" is their idea of normal sex, and it can include virtually any sex practice.

Question: Does Mountain Dew lower your sperm count?

Answer: Nope. That's an urban legend no doubt invented by a guy trying to convince a girl that she wouldn't get pregnant if they drank Mountain Dew. The stuff has no effect on sperm.

Question: Is it unsanitary to have a guy pee inside of you?

Answer: But, *why?* How did the subject come up? Has someone suggested that this is a fun, good thing to do as part of sex? Do you like this person? If so, *why?*

First off, if a guy has an erection and he is having intercourse with someone, that is, if his penis is in the vagina, urination is the farthest thing from his mind; he's working on ejaculating. Second, it is very hard to urinate under those circumstances, as the muscles that control urination are shutting off the bladder so you can ejaculate.

Now, the urine of a healthy person is about as close to sterile as anything the human body produces. If you don't have an STD or infection of some sort, it is clean enough that first aid field manuals recommend that it be used to wash wounds if you have nothing else at hand. However, no doctor is going to agree that urinating in the vagina is a good idea. It will change the pH (acidity) of the vagina, which can lead to various infections, and urine in the uterus, however unlikely, is probably not recommended.

Question: Would it hurt to put a string down your pea hole and pull it out?
Can you put finger in your penis hole

Answer: I'd tell you to go home and try it, with the assignment to let us all know how it went, but if you are dumb enough to ask the question, you may be dumb enough to do it. While we could all have fun laughing and pointing at your lameness, your parents might sue me and the school, so seriously dude, don't EVER try something this dumb. You could do serious damage to your penis and urethra pushing *anything* down (up?) there (with what instrument, I fear to ask) and pulling it back out. And, *duh!* it will hurt, *a lot!* Darwin Award for lameness, but a 10 for bad spelling, grammar and punctuation....

Question: Do boy cat's penises have teeth, or is it the other way around?

Answer: The male cat penis has a band of small "teeth" behind the head of the penis. After ejaculation, these small, one millimeter spines rake the inside of the female cat's vagina when the male withdraws, which stimulates the female cat to ovulate and leads to fertilization. Sounds grim, but it works for cats.

Question: Has anyone ever died during sex?

Answer: Of course. People, usually men, have had heart attacks, strokes, and the like during sex and have died. Not fun for their partner.

Question: Has anyone ever been electricuted on their penis.

Answer: Of course. If you can think of it, someone has tried it, or accidentally done it some way. Google "penis electrocution" and see what you get. You will be astounded. Young men, and some not so young, will do *anything* to stimulate their penis. Some of these things involve electricity, and turn out very badly.

Question: What kind of sickko would eat the afterbirth/placenta?
Would it be blasphemous to declare the menstrual fluids of an innocent woman as having healing powers? (same handwriting on both questions, different question slips – clearly a kid with wide ranging sexual and cultural interests.)

Answer: Through history, menstrual fluids from virginal women/girls and virginal girls in general have been associated with all sorts of religious and spiritual powers. As to whether it's blasphemy or not depends on what religion you believe in. It's only blasphemy if a particular religion says it is. Other religions may not care. There is certainly nothing medically or scientifically unusual about an "innocent" or virgin human female, and no scientific evidence they have special powers.

Actually, many if not most, animals do eat the placenta after giving birth. It has a lot of nutrients valuable to nursing mothers. Very few human cultures do so, but some do have recipes for cooking it, believing also that it is beneficial to the new mother. Certainly eating it raw is more than most people could face, and there is the danger of blood borne diseases.

Question: On Oprah, Dr. Oz said that a man will live longer having sex 4-5 times a week. Is this true?

Answer: Who am I to argue with Dr. Oz? If you saw the segment, Dr. Oz was saying that both the exercise of sex, combined with the stress reduction and the release of various hormones during sex, is beneficial to both sexes and can reduce the chances of heart disease, strokes, and other health issues for adults. This discussion was aimed primarily at middle age adults. Teenagers do not have the same health issues, and using this argument to get your girlfriend to have sex with you is bogus.

Question: Will you die if your penis like gets cut off?

Answer: It is possible to die of blood loss from cutting off the penis if the victim does not or cannot get immediate medical attention. With proper first aid (*duh! apply pressure and stop the bleeding!*), paramedics, and modern medical practice, it's not too likely.

Question: Why are there hairy condoms?

Answer: Where do you guys get this stuff? I did an internet search and could find nothing legit on the subject, just links for porn sites and the sale of questionable Chinese folk medicines. So, who knows?

Question: Why is it so hard to get semen out of hair: Why is skeet so sticky?

Answer: Normally, soap and water or shampooing do just fine, so I'm not sure what the problem is here, other than hygiene issues. Remember, the purpose of semen is to carry and protect the sperm inside the penis and vagina; it has no evolutionary purpose outside of those areas. It's sticky and gooey so it stays put and allows the sperm to get where they need to be. It is not made for your convenience or easy clean-up if you get it elsewhere. The obvious question is, what are you doing to get semen in your hair?

Question: If your dad gives you a porn mag is it ok to look at it?

Answer: How to answer that one? My natural reaction would be that the subject should be between you and your dad. My first question is "What do you mean by a porn mag?" There is a big difference between *Playboy* or *Maxim* compared to *Hustler* or some of the more hardcore publications out there. Pretty, naked women and reasonably well written articles are a whole different thing from hardcore sex photos and comics. My question would be, "Why is he doing this?" If the intent is to sit and talk you through this experience, explaining the real world implications of what sex is like for real people compared to what you see, it's not a bad thing. Certainly, I can't support giving you such a magazine without that conversation and guidance. Just turning you loose unguided with hardcore stuff at your age is only going to convey a mixed-up image of what sex is and/or should be, and I frankly think that would be wrong. I have real doubts that even with guidance this is a good idea at your age. What's the rush? I can only suggest that you talk it through with Dad and see what he's going for, but I have my doubts.

The point is, if your dad emphasizes that the sex you see in a hardcore porn magazine or online has almost nothing to do with what most people actually do sexually, and in particular, what most women and girls want in sex, then, and only then would I agree that it might possibly be a positive thing to do. But even then...

Question: Why do girls get their clit pierced?

Answer: Probably for the same reason that men get their penis pierced: because they can, because they like the way it looks, because someone they like likes the way it looks. People get pierced and tattooed everywhere these days. By the way, the clitoris itself is never pierced (unless someone makes a *big* mistake), but rather the little hood of skin over the clitoris. Piercing the clitoris itself would not only be **very** painful, but it quite likely could damage the nerves and sensations in the clitoris. Nobody wants that.

Question: Can you explain what a strap on penis and a vibrator is, please. What is a vibrator/pocket rocket?

Answer: Well, since you said please... A "strap on" is a leather or plastic harness that goes around the waist of a woman (usually, but men also may wear them if their penis can no longer get erect due to disease or injury) that is designed to hold a dildo over the woman's vulva where a penis would normally be in a man. A dildo is an artificial penis, always made of some sort of soft plastic nowadays. The strap on harness and dildo are used for sexual intercourse the way a biological penis would be.

A vibrator describes a huge range of sex toys that are designed to vibrate. The vibrations are for stimulating the clitoris in women, which is usually *very* effective in giving women orgasms quickly and easily. Vibrators are shaped in various ways, but mostly they follow the general shape and size of a penis, including some that are designed to operate in strap on harnesses. Vibrators usually have battery powered motors in them that operate the vibrating mechanism, but some kinds actually plug into the wall, and are also legitimately used for massage therapy. A "pocket rocket" is a name for a small battery powered vibrator that can easily be carried in a purse or a pocket.

Question: Is it weird that I watch a lot of gay porn?

Answer: More to the point, how is it that a 14 year old boy is watching a lot of porn of any kind? (*Note to parents: Seriously people, you have got to update your web access protection software.*) There is a lot of anecdotal and some clinical evidence that the sex and sexuality you discover at middle school age is the sexuality that you want/expect more or less for life. Unfortunately, especially for girls nowadays, that imprint on guys is coming from hardcore online porn. So, gay porn or not, watching a lot of porn is not a great thing for the people in your future sex life.

If you are watching a lot of gay porn, it means you like gay porn. It may or may not mean you are gay, bisexual, or just looking. If you are honest with yourself, *you* know what you like, and who you are attracted to, and you don't really need me to tell you. My point is that it isn't whether you are gay or not, it's that you are watching a lot of porn of any kind at an age where you form patterns for life. The things you are seeing and the patterns you are setting may not be good for your future partners, gay or straight. If my saying "stop it dude!" makes a difference, then stop it. Somehow I doubt it, unfortunately.

What you and anybody watching online porn, straight, gay or whatever, these days must realize is that it is manufactured fantasy. Most of what you see is not even physically possible without a lot of behind-the-scenes, off-camera set-up and preparation. It does not show you anything that resembles real-life sex for most people, and in particular, it has even less to do with what even the most adventurous young women want out of a sexual relationship. It does not mean that a woman might not want to try and find she genuinely enjoys some of those acts some of the time with someone she loves. Everyone has their own preferences and favorites, just like we do in food and music. But, if you go into any relationship with a woman thinking it's going to be like a porn video all or even most of the time, you are going to set yourself and the girl up for disappointment, anger, and resentment, and you will most likely wreck the relationship, whether it's just "hooking up" or a serious girlfriend. Real people and real women will not be treated that way, at least not indefinitely. Women really do need conversation, attention, and some indication that you see them as something other than a sex toy. Believe it—don't fight it, get over it—if you still doubt that elemental fact of female nature. That is the way they are made, and for good reason. Remember, their evolutionary job is to find a reliable mate for raising children. Porn stars are not what they are looking for in a guy, and most of the stuff you see in porn does not make them feel good about themselves. (36, 37)

Question: Can a pennis go in any whole of your body (again, pity the poor English teacher. Similar questions are asked about all the body orifices.)
Can you cum in a girls eyeball?
Can you have ear sex?
Can you get a girl pregnant if you engage through intercourse through the nose, mouth, ears and eyes
Is it possible to have sex in the nose.

Answer: Well, we've handled the vaginal, oral, and anal openings. So now you want to try all the other "holes ," by the way, spelled h-o-l-e-s: the nostrils, the navel, the eye (*seriously, the eye*?) Do you actually expect to find someone that will let you try to put your penis in their eye or nose? Do you think that *Family Guy,* while it is great comedy, was ever intended to be an accurate guide to good judgment in your sex life? Really? *(Note to reader: the Family Guy cartoon TV show had an episode with a running gag about using all the orifices in the body for sex, which of course means that a significant number of 14 year olds think it must be true.)*

Now, having dealt with the scary gullibility of people clearly not mature enough to get the humor of *Family Guy,* please do not try the only remaining hole, the ear. It is delicate, and if you are in dumb enough to try to put your penis in there and someone is dumb enough to let you try, you could in fact do some real damage to the ear drum, and the semen could contribute to an ear infection.

Let's have a show of hands. How many girls out there want to have some guy's penis in their eye, ear, or nose? What, no volunteers?..

As to pregnancy, none of these openings in any way connects to the reproductive organs. There will be no pregnancy, just massive embarrassment that you asked and tried these things.

One other thought. Again, if you *could* actually *fit* your penis into someone's nose or ear, wouldn't that just say something really embarrassing about the size of your penis? Think about it...

Deeply worried about our next generation's intellectual gene pool...

Question: If I get a boner in class, how do I hide it?

Answer: The curse of being a young dude: getting the unwanted erection at the wrong time. This happens to all men at one time or another. There is a video on various gossip sites of Jay-Z walking out of a restaurant with an obvious erection. Of course, he was walking out of the restaurant with his wife, Beyonce... It can cause you to remain seated when you would really like to get up, carry your books or backpack in odd ways, and try to casually turn your back on people while hoping they won't know what's up (Ha! *what's UP???!?!)* It's not fair because it just happens, even when sex is the farthest thing from your mind. Of course, once you have the erection, sex is then very much on your mind, and putting sex and your erection out of your mind so it will go away is almost impossible, and you're stuck with this tent pole in your pants.

One thing to consider: however cool you think it is to have your butt hanging out of your sagging pants, showing off your attractively plaid boxers, there is a lot to be said for boxer briefs in that they corral the penis and keep even the erect member pressed against your body so it is much less noticeable. Jock straps work well in this respect too. If you still insist on still rocking the lame, decades-old saggy pants and boxers gangsta look, you can wear a

ALL THE OTHER STRANGE, FREAK

jock or boxer briefs under the boxers to control the random erection. Short of that and focusing on your math problem or sentence diagramming, doing some slow breathing exercises to relax and letting some time pass, there is not much to be done. My sympathies...

Question: Why do porn stars use their first pet's name as their first name and the street they grew up on as their last?

Answer: They don't. Well, maybe someone did at some point, but this is just a party game because it makes for some funny, silly names, like many porn star names.

Porn stars, even more than regular actors, use made-up names so their families are not embarrassed by their work. It's fun to mess with. Mine would be Tuffy Petaluma, not a name I would want for porn or anything else.

Question: If I had sex with an ugly girl, will I start looking like her?

Answer: This question assumes that an ugly girl would actually want to have sex with you, which I wouldn't count on. Clearly someone failed 7th grade science and genetics, or you would remember that the *only* thing that affects your appearance is the genes that you were born with, and you got those genes from your parents. I noticed that the writer of this question checked off that he has in fact talked to his parents about the question. I'm dying to know how they answered. So, the "ugly" girl who had the bad taste to have sex with you would have no effect on your appearance.

SEXUAL HARASSMENT AND SEXUAL ASSAULT

These topics come up more and more among teenagers. Texting, sexting, and social network sites on the Internet have opened up a whole new world of ways to make someone miserable. Most people have heard of cases in the news of young people driven to suicide, assault, and murder by campaigns of harassment and hate on line. It's not a joke—which means many kids think it's just that. Of course, sexual harassment is not the same as sexual assault and rape. However, they both come under the umbrella of unwanted and illegal sexual attention, so we are going to deal with them here.

One of the most common misconceptions that people have about sexual harassment is that it is always guys harassing girls. While that relationship predominates, and probably always will, we increasingly see sexually aggressive young women harassing boys or other girls. The sexual boldness of some teenage girls is pretty jaw-dropping nowadays, and the sexting and posting they do through their phones and social web sites can be just as uncomfortable for boys as it traditionally has been for girls.

Questions: If my boyfriend keeps sending me a picture of his wang. I hate it. What is this?

If someone keeps bugging you about looking at something, and you tell them no but they still do it, is that a form of sexual harassment? (and it's a drawing or a picture)

Answer: These two questions are the very definition of sexual harassment. That is, the person still sends you the pictures after you have clearly told them to stop. Now, telling him to stop cannot be a playful sounding "tee-hee, stop it you silly"" I must be a straight, loud, and clear, "dude, I hate this and if you care about me you will stop it!" What this means is that pretty much any crass thing someone says to you or sends you is fun and games and lame nonsense until you say to **stop**. When you have clearly said stop, and the penis pictures or whatever he or she does of a sexual nature that you hate continues, it then legally crosses over into sexual harassment, and the person committing those acts can get in serious legal trouble. You can file a police complaint, the person can be arrested, and you can get a restraining order. Not all of those things necessarily can or need to happen immediately in any given situation, but those are the legal remedies available to someone being sexually harassed.

Very simply, a clear, unambiguous message (something in writing is always good as it helps any legal situation that may follow) that you want the behavior to stop means the whole legal status of the relationship has changed. It means that any further continuation of the unwanted sexual behavior *is now classified as sexual harassment.*

I would also suggest you need to seriously think about calling this person a boyfriend. Surely you can do much better.

Question: How do you prevent rape?

Answer: That's a tough one, in that the circumstances vary so much.

First, what is rape? Rape is forcing a sex act on someone against their will. That is, forcefully inflicting a sex act of any kind, manual, oral or penetrating the vagina or anus without their direct permission. We are **not** talking about "rape fantasy" sex games that a couple may play, because then it's not really rape as both people have consented to play out the fantasy. And just because someone expresses an interest in such a fantasy, no one has the right to rape them and justify it as fulfilling that person's fantasy. *Again, any sex against someone's will is rape.*

Keep in mind _most—75% in most studies—rape is actually committed by a guy the girl knows, not by some stranger_ that grabs her and drags her into an alley. You've probably heard the term "date rape." This refers to someone who forces their girl-friend or date to have sex without her consent. Obviously, these two people on a date know each other on some level, yet the sex is still forced. _Again, this is in fact **by far** the most common type of rape._

Date rape is harder to prosecute because the people know each other and may even be close, so the incident quickly becomes a "he said /she said" situation where one person's word is pitted against the other. If there are signs of bruising and forcible pen-etration of the vagina, the case is helped. If the girl was drugged, as often happens, the forcible aspects may also be absent, unless she gets a blood test soon enough after the rape to verify the pres-ence of the drug in her blood. Because of the difficulty in verifying these cases, most incidents of date rape unfortunately go un-re-ported, and many girls and women chalk them up to experience. This shouldn't be, but many women consider it a fact of life.

How to prevent it? Know who you are going out with. Try to have some knowledge of the person's reputation from your friends. Know that people are not always who they seem on Facebook, and even if you check them out there are no guarantees, though as you would expect, most guys are quite decent.

My co-author and wife (and yes, I have permission to share this) once went on a date set up by a close, very conservative married friend. The date was by all accounts a "nice," professional, all-around good guy. They had a nice evening, and at the end, he insisted Fran visit his apartment before he took her home to her apartment. They guy's roommate was home, and Fran figured nothing was to come of it. She had a drink the guy fixed for her, and literally, the next thing she knew, the sun was up the following morning and the "nice" guy was on top of her having sex with her. From the guilty look on the roommate's face, she was pretty sure he had had sex with her too during the night. Her date took her home, apologized, and asked if they could go out again!!

Now, this was over 35 years ago, before the widespread awareness of date rape drugs and the huge reforms that have taken place in police policy toward sex crimes. Frannie didn't report it or tell anyone about it; there was no point at that time as there was no way to prove anything. Further, the police and most everyone else at that time assumed that if you went to a guy's place, you had in effect consented to have sex. So aside from avoiding getting seriously drunk (not that you should be getting drunk at all at your age), ALWAYS make sure you keep an eye on whatever drink you have to make sure it is not drugged. These things still happen too often, and a drunk or drugged girl or woman is still considered fair game for individual or gang rape by many young men, as a number of recent teenage/party/drunken girl rape trials attest.

Bad as date rape is, the thing that terrifies most women is forcible rape by a stranger. There is no assault that one person can commit on another that can make someone feel more powerless, helpless, terrified, and betrayed than forcible rape. When you add the real or implied threat of death that almost always figures into rape cases, it's hardly surprising that this fear is one of the most deep-seated in women.

How to avoid it? Common sense goes a long way towards improving your odds. First, don't act like a victim. Research done with rapists shows that they tend to look for women who appear weak, fearful, and vulnerable. Don't be that chick. Walk confidently, with friends. Look people in the eye. Avoid walking or jogging alone in the dark and near places like alleys and isolated, obscured areas with overgrown plants and places to hide. Many colleges and even high schools have after-hours safety escort services that will walk a girl to her car. If you have concerns about the area where you live, windows should be shut at night (tough in the summer time, I know), and of course, the home locked. Keep car doors locked at all times. A legal can of pepper spray can be worth a lot.

There are many rape prevention and self-defense classes available at community centers, junior colleges, and even churches and synagogues nowadays. These can help a lot in terms of building confidence, self-knowledge, and teaching ways to avoid trouble. My daughters both took the Krav Maga martial arts training. This is the Israeli armed forces' self-defense program, and it is no nonsense, take-them-down approach. My older daughter became very proficient, and I pity the guy that attacks her with anything less than a loaded gun he knows how to use. The bottom line: do anything you can to avoid coming under the physical control of the would -be rapist.

Yet that raises another issue. Most self-defense course teach you to run like hell, scream, fight, and do anything to attract attention and avoid being dragged into a car or somewhere you cannot be helped. This is excellent advice, as most rapists are looking for a quiet, compliant victim. However, most police, male and female, will advise that if you have been captured, that is, are under the physical control of a rapist, *and* he has a deadly weapon, your situation has changed dramatically, and active, physical resistance can get you killed. Your circumstances have changed from avoiding rape to avoiding death. Compliance and making some sort of emotional connection with the rapist is probably the safest course, awful as that may seem.

Avoiding rape calls for common sense. You cannot live in fear your whole life, yet the fact is nearly one in four women experience some sort of sexual assault in life. Statistics for the kind of forcible rape all women fear show that the crime is declining. Again, most rape is date rape, and you just have to use your head in party situations. That's also why parents worry about their daughters at parties. Nice boys get caught up in dumb ideas and nice girls have bad things happen to them at nice homes with nice people.

Men get raped too, more often than many people realize. It's common in prison, but can happen in hazing or initiation practices in some teams or gangs, and sometimes in the same random, violent manner that women are raped. It can be at least as emotionally and physically devastating for men as it is for women because people accept that these things can happen to women but, "not to any man who calls himself a man."

The "rape culture" exists unacknowledged just below the surface of many cultures around the world, including our own. It is much less about sex than it is about power, domination and humiliation of the victim. Even if people don't say it out loud, there is a sense that the victim, male or female deserved or brought on what happened to them. It is one of the deepest, darkest parts of human nature that modern cultures try to suppress and surpass, with varying degrees of success. Make no mistake about it, rape of any kind is a violent attack on the physical and emotional well being of any human. There can never be any justification for it in any civilized society, and it inevitably represents the very worst of us.

Question: When you are raped can you get pregnant?

Answer: Yes, of course, unfortunately. Despite the confusion on this topic by some members of Congress, millions of women are raped all over the world every year in wars, by "friends," or by strangers. Many get pregnant. If you are ovulating and a viable sperm gets to the egg, you can get pregnant; it doesn't matter how the sperm got there.

Question: Is it painful when a woman is being raped?

Answer: Yes, it usually is. Given that the woman is fearful, often taken by surprise, tense, and certainly NOT sexually aroused, she is not going to be relaxed and lubricated. Forceful penetration under these circumstances is almost always painful, and usually results in some abrasion, bruising and damage to the vagina.

AND THEN, SOME QUESTIONS JUST STAND ALONE...

Question: Can you aim your ejaculation

Is it possible for your testicles to go into your stomach and come out of your mouth (from some Kung fu movie???)

If you ejaculated on a girl on her vagina from distances up to 30 feet and the sperm goes in will the baby be deformed?

Would you cut your dick off for 10 million dollars?

What is the best time for sex?

Would it be smart to put icy-hot in your anal canal? (I sooo hope he tried it...)

WHAT DOES IT ALL MEAN, AND WHAT, IF ANYTHING, CAN WE DO ABOUT IT?

So, where does the above leave us, and what do I believe we can glean from the questions being asked by middle schoolers?

Restatement of my first sweeping statement: while many of us are aware of how sexualized our culture has become, most have no idea how pervasive, universal, accepted, and "natural" sexuality is for the current generation of young people growing to adulthood. It surrounds every aspect of their being: their music, their clothes, the TV, Webcasts, music videos, video games, podcasts and downloads they watch, the movies they see, the magazines they read, their social networking websites and the gossip among friends. Even those baby boomers who grew up leading the sexual revolution in the 60's, 70's, and 80's did not experience a world where sexuality was so universal that the idea of opting out doesn't even necessarily come to mind for many young people. There is only a limited amount that parents can do to control and police this, short of joining a cult in a compound. Consider:

- *Revisit the statement from the opening paragraph of this book in the introduction. For under 18 year-olds (both boys **and** girls), the fourth and fifth most searched terms on the Internet are "Sex" and "Porn." "Boobs" and "Pussy" are well up in the top 100. (1)*
- *From listening to students, it is apparent to me that too many parents are lax on maintaining their Web access restricting software that supposedly keeps their kids from porn sites, **the source of a great many of the questions above from boys and girls**. Even if they do keep up with this chore, it is not unusual for the software to be hacked, often by your very internet/tech-savvy children, or they will see the content anyway at a friend's house where the parents are more permissive (or clueless), that is less than Internet secure.*
- *You can block channels on TV but they can see those shows at the same friend's house.*
- *You can drop them off at the multiplex to see the PG movie, where they have refined the art of theater hopping and will see the R rated sexual slasher movie instead, followed by days of detailed discussion of the key points in the movie with friends who did and didn't see the film.*
- *The exposed, shaved or unshaved crotch-shot adventures, intended or not, of any number of young celebrities are on the evening entertainment news shows, with all the pictures you need a few clicks away on the 'net. Now, most of the girls I talk to turn up their noses at the gross stupidity of these antics, but it's out there, setting the "anything goes" sexual atmosphere.*
- *"Sexting!" The girl who flashes her breasts at a pool party Saturday will find photos of her exposed flesh stored on the cellphone of every boy in the school district by the start of church on Sunday, and followed by their appearance on*

viral child porn sites by Monday. Actually, it will probably happen faster than that. A girl or guy sends erotic cellphone photos to the newfound love of their lives, only to have them shared with the world when the relationship angrily breaks up for all the reasons middle school romances break up. This happened at least a couple of times in our school district, and it's hardly a stretch to imagine the experience was anything but unique. Yes, she's underage and it's illegal, but it's irretrievably out there in the web universe, essentially forever, and you can bet your life that it's on the innumerable kiddie-porn websites providing masturbatory entertainment to pedophile lowlifes from a couple doors down on your block to Kazakhstan. As organic as the web is to kids, many do not begin to get how fast bad stuff spreads, or where it can go.

- *If those pictures are sent to her father, mother or teachers (let alone her college entrance board some years later), all these adults will be guilty of possessing child pornography, whether they received the images voluntarily or not. Now the likelihood of real prosecution is low, but it could mean some uncomfortable interviews with some skeptical detectives and a few expensive billable hours with a lawyer.*
- *For that matter, try buying your daughters clothes some summertime that you would have been let out of the house with at her age. It's hard not to dress your daughter like a teenage hooker fantasy creature, especially if she has some say in the matter.*

My intent is not to be alarmist, though many of my observations may be alarming. I am *not* leading a charge for some new legislation or morality movement; far from it. That ship has sailed, and this is the culture we live in. I'll leave such (usually) misguided crusades to others. My intent is to amuse, but also give us pause so that we help our young people deal with the realities of the modern world. The combination of teen bravado and the image of effortless, consequence-free sexuality that pervades our culture can cost a kid a lot before they figure it out. ***Especially girls...*** We all have to figure sex out for ourselves anyway, but the more guarded world that most of us grew up in gave us time to mature to some extent before we were thrust (loaded word there) into the adult sexual world. Young people today are almost precluded from that option, so a realistic understanding of the culture and its impact on the sexualization of younger people is vital.

Further, they are by no means all "doing it," but a surprising (or shocking) number (most studies and surveys put the number at 10 to 20% of 12 to 14 year olds are sexually active) are experimenting.

This experimentation starts in middle school (despite the occasional horror stories in the news, it's still pretty rare even among mature fifth graders), usually avoiding standard penis-in-vagina sex. Instead, there is a lot of manual, oral, or anal experimentation. They are smart enough to get that this largely (sperm stray, and accidents happen, however) avoids pregnancy and has the further benefit of being able to claim, with a straight face, "I'm still a virgin daddy!"

Indeed, teenage girls are at the nexus of this culture shift, and much of what we try to do is to bring this realization home to both girls **and** boys.

With that in mind, I've begun starting my Family Life unit by putting the following statements up in a brief, simple PowerPoint:

1. Wishful thinking – that is, self-deception—is the root of all evil.
2. This all comes down harder on girls than guys, but a significant proportion of girls are remarkably, frighteningly

(given the higher potential cost of careless sexual activity to girls) sexually aggressive in our current culture.

3. Murphy's Law is real and waiting to mess with your life.

4. The Center for Disease Control (CDC) recently conducted a survey that found that one in four American teenage girls had a sexually transmitted disease by age 18: ***ONE IN FOUR*** (28)

5. While many parents are in denial, young guys are forming their impressions and desires about sex from early exposure to online porn, starting in the middle school years and even earlier. The problem is that sex for most people, and girls/women in particular, has little to do with the sadomasochistic sexual world depicted in modern porn, but that very porn world is what young boys and men expect in their sexual relationships, starting in middle school. This feeds items 1 - 4 above.

6. And finally, their brains aren't done yet. If you've followed any of the literature on brain development over the last couple decades, you realize that young people do the insanely stupid, reckless, what-could-you-possibly-have-been-thinking-oh-wait-clearly-nothing-like-thinking-could-possibly-have-been-going-on things they do simply because the frontal lobe of their brains isn't done growing and the software is faulty. That is, the very part of our brains that thinks about risk and consequences and tells us "wait a minute, this could go really badly" simply isn't fully there yet, and won't be for some years. It's worse for boys: girls get there often in their middle teens, while boys often don't develop this part of their brains and the thinking skills to go with it until well into their twenties (hence the insurance rates you pay for boy drivers, and their domination of the crime and lameness statistics). You simply cannot realistically expect them to make common sense

decisions, especially on the spur of the moment when hormones are dominating their lives. This simple fact of human maturing—intuitively understood by all cultures for thousands of years—explains much of the silliness and tragedy of youth as well as the institutions, both legal and customary, that we put in place to protect kids.

Here's where I lead the discussion with each of these observations:

Wishful thinking... The late, great science fiction author Robert Heinlein's character Lazarus Long once cautioned, "Never underestimate the power of human stupidity." Another great sci-fi author, Douglas Adams (*The Hitch-hikers Guide to the Galaxy*) cogently observed that, "Human beings, who are almost unique in having the ability to learn from the experience of others, are also remarkable for their apparent disinclination to do so." This innate quirk of humanity is nowhere more highly developed than in the teenager, virtually all of whom seem to express a gene that tells them 1) They are invulnerable, and anything bad will happen to someone else; 2) No adult knows as much about life, especially *their* life as they do; and 3) Only their generation could have invented sex; nobody old enough to be a teacher or parent could possibly understand the subject (except for the icky realization that each of their parents had to have had sex at least once). This trait is of course one of the things that make young people amazing and heroic and able to attempt and succeed at things older and wiser heads think "impossible." But most of us know from bitter experience that acting like something is true *because we want it to be that way (wishful thinking or self-deception) rather than the way it really is,* is the true source of most of life's unhappiness, whether it be romance, finance, or politics. Certainly contracting sexually transmitted diseases, and virtually all unplanned pregnancies, result almost entirely from "wishing and hoping" rather than sensible preparation. (28, 29)

This all comes down harder on girls... This one arose from conversations with my wife (we are parents of two daughters now in their 20's and 30's as of this writing) and independently through talks with a highly protective, but realistic mother of one of my girl students. Both were concerned that with the questions mostly coming from boys during family life, combined with girls' natural reluctance to draw attention to themselves in public and in matters of sex, that much of the impact of young sexuality on girls would be lost or glossed over. The points made sense and I resolved to focus on this issue. I try to make the following items clear to kids:

Sex happens with and to two people. For guys, hopefully, it's is the dawning of the realization that it's not all about getting off, and that both your life and the girl's can and will be profoundly affected by sex. However, no matter what, everything about sex and sexuality is more involved for girls/women. Why? How?

Women are designed to get pregnant. Boys/men are designed to get them pregnant. That is the basic species survival point of sex, all else aside. I tell guys that pregnancy will never happen to you. On the other hand, pregnancy or the prospect of it affects every aspect of a woman's body, hormones, and mental outlook. I point out to girls that if they pay attention to their body, those times of the month where they feel most "horny" and more willing to say "just this one time," happen when they are ovulating, and therefore its exactly the time they are most likely to conceive. Their hormones program them that way.

Girls get periods. We of course avoid the quaint Biblical use of the term "the curse," but I ask guys to consider their outlook if they had to bleed from their penis a few days to a week every month with all the paraphernalia connected with that, while the rest of the month their mood would constantly change as your body hormonally prepares to get pregnant.

Germs of all kinds prefer warm, wet places. Girls have warm, wet places that guys don't have. Girls get sexually transmitted diseases more easily than guys, and it's often harder for them to notice that they have them.

Childbirth is no picnic. A lot of people blame the movie "Juno" for loosening the attitude toward teen pregnancy. I don't agree with that. I felt the movie showed clearly what the pregnancy and childbirth cost Juno in every frame. It was Juno herself who realized that as her condition advanced she had become the "cautionary whale" at school. When it comes down to the act of childbirth, I point out that most women who have delivered conventionally compare it to having a bowel movement with a watermelon. That metaphor usually elicits some satisfying winces, moans, and giggles.

Our culture still expects women take on primary responsibility for pregnancy and disease prevention. Women have to take the pill (which hormonally mimics pregnancy, with similar risks for many women) or wear an IUD, which has its own set of risks and discomforts. Efforts to develop a male pill are halting, both for technical/medical reasons and because we probably don't put the cultural effort into something that many men openly or unconsciously feel threatens their masculinity. Similarly, many experienced, adult men, let alone boys, resist or refuse wearing condoms, and young vulnerable girls who want love and attention (*and* sex) can find it hard to stand their ground on this point, especially since boys have available to them girls who don't insist.

While few want our culture to go back to the purely paternalistic worldview that women should be protected property in pioneer dresses, I am reminded of another of sci-fi author Robert Heinlein's quotes, this from the perspective of his character, Lazarus Long, a 2000 year old man, some 2000 years in the future: "Whenever women have insisted on absolute equality with men, they have invariably wound up with the dirty end of the stick. What they are and what they do makes them superior to men, and their proper tactic is to demand special privileges, all the traffic will bear. They should never settle merely for equality. For women, 'equality' is a disaster." (27)

A girl with self-respect, self-knowledge, and a real world understanding of sex and sexuality, who both understands the power her sexuality gives her as well as what it can cost her socially, personally and physically, is a lot less likely to be a sexual victim or to let low self-esteem make her do things that are unhealthy. We have to nurture that balance of understanding, because the social construct that protected girls by shaming them into avoiding sex has largely vanished, and has yet to be replaced by something more positive, fulfilling, and self-sustaining. Today, I fear that the pressure on young women to be sexual athletes and toys, to be sexually compliant, eager "young men with vaginas" *and* have a career *and* raise kids, often alone outside a committed family that supports the needs of men *and* women *and* children, may be the unintended consequence of demanding the life options that women always in fact deserved to have. Hopefully, in the lifetime of our middle school sons and daughters, we can grow some balance out of the present reality. Probably they will. Remember: our parents thought the hippies of the 60s and 70s heralded the end of civilization. Many hippies are now conservative investment bankers and overprotective grandparent members of the PTA.

One aspect of this is the remarkable sexual aggressiveness of a significant portion of the teenage girl population. If you doubt it, check out the intensely physical nature of flirting on the part of girls nowadays, and the jaw-dropping stripper pole antics of girls at a school dance. Studies have shown that there is actually little difference in the baseline libido of men and women. We have culturally protected women (and young men) from their libidos by teaching them to restrain it, while the realities of pregnancy and disease historically enforced these cultural norms ruthlessly. When the culture removes pregnancy as a daily concern and makes many diseases preventable and treatable, the cultural constraints on girl's libidos are largely removed. In fact, our culture, through advertisements, movies, television, and the Internet tells girls daily to be sexually available, pliable, and in fact to aggressively pursue sexual connection. In recent years there has been a remarkable shift in the question box questions I get from girls (and yes, I can tell they are from girls due to the perfect feminine handwriting, the little circles and hearts dotting the "i's," and the first person, feminine "I" in the questions, like "If I give my boyfriend a blowjob...") address specific sex acts and how to perform then, something I used to get only from the most brazen, smart ass boys. Girls and women have a right to fulfilling sex life, just like anyone else. But sex still and always will have a potentially higher cost for women. Girls need to be armed with a real world understanding of what awaits them.

Murphy's Law... (what can go wrong will go wrong, sooner or later) is real and is waiting to mess with your life. This is the flip side extension of wishful thinking. Bad stuff happens, and you are a fool if you don't think about and prepare for it.

Many kids actually get that they have to take precautions. Many boys and girls do in fact dutifully obtain condoms and use them if they have sex. Many girls do go on the pill, often with their mother leading the way. Yet despite these forays into responsible adult approaches to sex, they are still kids, they don't always do the right thing every time. Having taken these preventive measures, the ugly possibility that the precautions may fail, simply cannot and will not be considered because that can't happen to them. Bad stuff only happens to sluts and bad people. And of course, there are the famous last words "Just this once." So, the next big club you have to hit them with is:

WHAT DO YOUR DO WHEN YOU GET PREGNANT OR GET AN STD ANYWAY??!!

- *Are the two of you (this is NOT just the girl's problem!) pre-pared to terminate a pregnancy? Terminate means abortion.*
- *Will your personal morals or religion allow you to do that?*
- *If so, where, who, and how will the two of you get the abortion and pay for it?*
- *If you keep the child, will the two of you put it up for adoption or raise the baby?*
- *Who will help the two of you raise, pay for, get medical treatment for, feed, clothe, and educate the baby?*

Okay, so you didn't get pregnant, you "only" got an STD. What then?

- *How, where, who will the two of you get to treat it—that's right, if you've got it your partner does. Either they gave it to you, or you gave it to them, and anyone else they/you had sex with probably has it. Who is going to tell your friends to get checked and treated? Who pays?*
- *If you get one of the permanent, incurable STDs like herpes, HPV, or HIV, are you ready to tell and protect anyone you have sex with in the future about your condition?*

These aren't scare tactics. These are the everyday realities that real world adults have to consider every time they have sex with someone new. Many adults don't get it right. If you are scared by these facts, that's normal. It's scary, and if you don't want to deal with all this all the time that's fine. You're a kid and you shouldn't have to at this point in your life. But then be honest with yourself and realize that you are not ready to have sex if you can't face up to these facts and live your life accordingly.

The Center for Disease Control (CDC) have done studies over the last decade or so that show that by the age of 18 (that's in the next 4 to 5 years for your middle schooler), one in four American girls with have some form of STD. ***ONE IN FOUR!! BY THE TIME THEY LEAVE HIGH SCHOOL!!*** (28)

Now, you can put whatever spin on that fact you want and do calculations about how many kids are having sex and how many of those having sex are catching STDs, but so what? It also no doubt means that at least that many boys have an STD. The thing is, it's much easier for boys to notice they have some bug affecting their beloved penis and they are more likely to get it treated because they notice it, and also because there is less stigma attached to guys getting an STD. Bottom line: there are way too many young people having unprotected sex way too early in their life, and, as usual, it hits girls harder. Parent response? You better start having an in-depth sex talk earlier than you expect (as well as demanding modern, science based sex education from your schools), and you better get the girls and boys in your family the human papillomavirus vaccine before middle school.

The availability of on line hard core porn is radically distorting the image and expectations of sex and sexuality in young men and boys starting in or even before middle school. This is another genie that's very hard to put back in the bottle, but parents have got to wrestle with it on several levels.

It's easy for this to be one of those "not my kid" issues that parents turn a blind eye to. Now, my biggest rant is against wishful thinking on the part of parents and kids, but it's hard to blame someone who doesn't want to visualize their 12 year old watching what's available on the web these days. The fact is, it's ridiculously easy to find *any* kind of porn videos or stills, for free, with just a few keystrokes. For a few dollars a month, endless hours of mind-bending, eye-watering porn can be viewed by anybody. Parents who are diligent about maintaining their Internet access software are subverted by tech-savvy kids who hack the software, or failing that, their sons (and daughters) view the same content at via a college age brother, cousin, creepy uncle, or friend with oblivious, blasé parents.

Please be clear that I am not campaigning against porn. Like most vices, porn should be available to responsible adults. However, like those other vices (liquor, driving, smoking and drugs), we need a whole infrastructure of legal and cultural norms to protect kids from them until they have some chance of handling them in some kind of rational adult fashion. Let's face it; many adults don't handle many of those vices well.

What I try to convey to kids is that what they see in porn has almost nothing to do with what normal, adult, healthy people do for sex, at least most of the time. Further, if boys expect their teenage girlfriend, or any woman, to supply them with those acts all time on demand as a matter of course in their eventual sex life, they are going to make themselves and the girl deeply unhappy. Further, in keeping with the thesis that all this falls harder on girls, young women need to understand that they are not automatically required to perform like a porn star from the get-go in any relationship. They have choices, whether they realize it or not.

Yet this is the sexual world faced by kids today. Boys grow up thinking virtually any sex act is a commodity to be provided by girls early and often in a relationship because that's the sex they see and experience online. Girls feel increasing pressure to provide these acts, because their boyfriends (or the boys they would like for a boyfriend) expect it, and if he doesn't get it from her, there are any number of girls who will willingly do so.

This not to say that that all your daughters are out there providing hand jobs, oral, and anal sex on demand. "Everyone lies about sex" (another Heinlein quote), and there can be a lot more talk than action, and a lot of them are still very much at the "eew-www" stage. I *am* saying that you would be surprised at how many are performing these acts, and more to the point, **you should be deeply concerned about the pressure the rest of the girls who are <u>not</u> engaging in these acts feel to provide them with.**

By the same token, not all of your sons are watching porn online all the time, but very few of them reach high school, let alone college, without seeing a fair amount of it somewhere. And, being young guys, their minds seethe with the continuously revolving trio of obsessions common to all young men: *Food, Sex* and *Explosions*, randomly, in no particular order, all the time. In current American culture, the sex obsession gets fed and formed by online porn, along with overall *Gossip Girl/90210/ Vampire Diaries/Jersey Shore/Skins/Spring Breakers* culture of assumed, consequence-free sexual availability. Even though *not* everyone is doing it, the cultural assumption on the part of teenagers, based on what they hear in their culture at school, and what they see in the media and the world around them, is that everyone else **really is doing it**, except them, and sooner or later they might as well join the party.

HOW DO YOU RESPOND AS
A PARENT -- OR A STUDENT?

As noted before, the current American culture is a very tough genie to put back in the bottle. We are a nation founded by Puritans who have created a sexually permissive culture that the most libertine elite of ancient Rome or 18th century Paris could only have dreamed of. We want our children's upbringing to be innocent in the best sense of the word, but we immerse them in the most pervasively sexual culture ever devised by human endeavor. The contrarian, Puritanical roots of American culture seek to protect "innocence" and deny the reality of our sexualized culture and basic human nature.

You can't have it both ways. You have to live in the culture we have, and you have to realistically prepare your children for life in that world. It doesn't mean you need to abandon your morals, religion, or family values. Nor does it mean you live in walled compound, grow beards, and clothe your women in burkas or pioneer dresses. It does mean you have no choice anymore but to arm your kids with knowledge of what they are getting into. You can't tell yourself that your kid has been raised in the church and has values that will prevent them doing something dumb. There are too many kids out there with purity rings and promise certificates that are turning up with STDs and pregnancies. In fact, a number of studies show that kids who sign up for these programs are at statistically higher risk for pregnancy and STDs because they deny to themselves what they are getting into when they do inevitably become sexually active at some point and don't take the precautions they might otherwise because that means they have to acknowledge to themselves what they are doing. Wishful thinking again. The flip side is that programs that stress abstinence *in addition to* pregnancy and STD information and prevention *and the consequences of irresponsible behavior* seem to clearly delay sexual activity and negative behaviors.

When you compare the rate of teen pregnancy, STDs, abortion, and condom/contraception use between the U.S. and Britain (which, as our parent country has similar conflicting approaches to sexuality and sex education) and the western European countries like France, Germany, and the Netherlands, the numbers are inescapable. See the graphs below for details. Very simply, France/Germany/Netherlands have rates in all the above categories that are fractions of the U.S rates. If you hate abortion, you should love in-depth sex education, because those "permissive" western European cultures have far fewer abortions among teens than Americans do. The fact is, if you understand sex, sexuality, and contraception in a real world context, there is very little excuse for getting pregnant or contracting STDs. Pregnancy and disease almost always result from ignorance and wishful thinking. (31: *Seriously, go to the link in the bibliography and check out this data!*)

So, my advice, and the thesis driving this book, is simple. Raise your kids with the best values you and your beliefs dictate. Take them to church, synagogue, mosque, or temple. Have them join prayer groups or raise them with the best of secular humanism values. The fact is, the core values of any culture, religious or secular, are remarkably the same, more or less coming down to the

Golden Rule. But then, earlier than you probably ever thought or desired (how many of you had your first serious crush, make-out session, or sexual experience at some church camp, youth group, or conference, right?..) make it clear to them that sexual activity carries great responsibility along with its great joys.

There is no moral hypocrisy here. You are not telling your children "no" on one hand and then giving them permission to have sex on the other. On the contrary, by combining the moral guidance and upbringing of your religious or cultural beliefs while providing them with the real world facts about their true nature as humans and the adult culture they will live in, usually far before they are really adult, you are giving them the tools they need to live their life both morally *and* safely. I fervently believe to do otherwise is to stunt them and set them up for heartbreak and failure.

The responsibilities of sexuality include:

1. Understanding that two lives are involved, and, in the case of STDs, the lives of everyone they have sex with the rest of their lives can be affected.
2. The same is true for babies. *Conceiving* a child is an act of selfish creation (or carelessness) *and* the species imperative of passing on one's genes. *Raising* a child is or should be one of the most selfless acts a person takes on. It is a 20 year responsibility for making the new baby a functional, happy contributor to society. The birth of a child completely changes one's life, even if it is given up for adoption. If that fact is not clearly, innately part of your world view, you have no business having children. Few 14 year olds have, or can be expected to have, this outlook.
3. Accidentally getting pregnant, or getting an STD in our modern age given what is known about preventing either occurrence, is almost always the result of ignorance,

wishful thinking or, and I'm being really charitable, bad luck. Teens are especially good at wishful thinking (which isn't, but can look a lot like stupidity), which comes from the fact that their brains are not finished growing yet, especially the part that thinks about consequences and bad outcomes. Nevertheless, the STD/Pregnancy statistics from Western European countries where in-depth sex education is the norm for youngsters are much lower than the American and English statistics, both nations with a similar, schizophrenic approach to sex ed. Your kids must have it drilled into them the mantra of this book: **If you can't or won't face the responsibilities of protecting yourself and your partner, you have no business having sex until you can !** And then make sure you and/or your school district provides that education. *In most districts in modern America, that responsibility falls on the parent. It's just too controversial for most school boards and most parent communities to face.* (24, 25)

4. Get your *boys and girls* vaccinated with Guardicil[tm] or whatever human Papillomavirus (HPV) vaccines become available. This is one of the few STDs that can be headed off with a vaccination. HPV is one of the most common STDs, and it is permanent. The spiking rate of oral and throat HPV warts and cancers, plus its long-known link to cervical cancer, makes this a must. I don't have specific data to support it, but kids are almost certainly more likely to have unprotected oral sex than they are penis-in-vagina sex. So are adults, because the pregnancy issue goes away. The oral HPV and cancer statistics certainly point to that. Do this immediately, and before middle school if possible. Keep in mind that Guardicil[tm] only covers the half dozen or so most common HPV strains, not all of them.

Like anything else in sexual activity, the vaccine does not remove the need for safer sex practices like condoms.

5. Girls have a right to their sexuality and sexual enjoyment. Nevertheless, the prospect of pregnancy and the greater risks of disease make the potential costs of sexuality inevitably higher for girls/women than for men and boys. A 14 year old girl in love for the first time almost certainly will not always put all that together. They must be armed with their options, however, and obviously, choosing no sex for now is one to be actively encouraged. However, she also needs to be aware of how to use and obtain birth control, condoms, medical treatment and the very practical option of ***masturbation***.

You want me to tell my little girl to masturbate??!!

This is not the perverted rant of a creepy male science teacher in late middle age. Please check out sex researcher and adviser Dr. Laura Berman's thoughtful advice on having "the talk" with young teenage girls and her suggestion that masturbation for girls can at least help head off a lot of hormone-driven romantic trouble. Boys are encouraged and expected to do it for sexual relief, yet we avoid letting girls in on the practical release of masturbation, fearing where it may lead. Trust me, kids and parents, not masturbating can lead to much worse. (27)

The fact is, the initial sexual relationships most teenage girls have are extremely one-sided affairs driven by the boy's needs and desires. Ask any woman about their first sexual experiences and relationships. They may have been exciting, even romantic, but few would say they were sexually or emotionally satisfying in the way any healthy adult woman would expect. Many sexually active girls spend their teens in a series of what are innocently abusive sexual experiences, servicing boys, driven by their very real feminine need to connect emotionally and the hope that sex with boys they like will give them that connection. What most of them actually get until they mature and wise up is used and dropped and gossiped about. Their own emotional and sexual needs are ignored by boys who don't care, of if they do care, are too clueless and inexperienced to help. All this is made worse when they start too young.

As noted in my discussion of question box inquiries, a shocking number of them don't even understand their clitoris or the idea of masturbation, let alone demanding equal, respectful attention to that unique organ and their own sexual needs if they do have sex with a boy. If they are having sex in their early-mid teens, it's about the boys, not about a real two-way sexual relationship, because in most cases they simply don't know that it can and should be any other way. Girls need to have this firm grounding in the raw medical facts and the common sense cultural knowledge of the centuries if they are to have the self-knowledge to be emotionally, physically, and socially healthy in today's world. Ultimately, it is the parent who creates that outlook, and that's Dr. Berman's point in her advice about empowering girls not only with the "facts of life" but with real knowledge of their bodies and their options outside of seeking a boy's attention by one-sidedly sexually pleasing him alone.

6. Boys need to be reintroduced to the idea of respect for the female sex. I am alarmed for girls, and I believe what I say about how sexuality is inevitably a greater burden on them. Please know that I also get the agony of being a middle school boy, and the whiplash of this congenital sexual drive/addiction that kicks in and replaces our brain with our penis. Okay, it's not a clinical addiction, but the only way to explain to girls and women why we men are the way we are is that some time in these middle school years

this sex thing kicks in and it just crowds out and displaces the innocent, bloodthirsty pursuits of boyhood with this obsession with girls (or whoever...), their body parts, and what we might get to do with them. It's not that we just see girls as sex toys; it's that we see them as these wonderful, exasperating human *others* that have all this wonderful sexual equipment attached. And it is *relentless,* messing with our minds and decision-making for much of our adult lives. Like I said above, *food, sex* and *explosions* dominate young male brains, and the sex part just gets out of hand. While girls owe us nothing because of this hormonal addiction, they do need to understand its power and the effect they have on males because of their power. Respect our male, ego-driven fragility as girls demand that we respect you as people and not just sex toys.

7. Boys, whatever is going on in your body, you do not have the right to be a jerk, or to impose your hormone driven jerkiness on girls or whoever if the object of your romantic/lustful/obsession. These feelings will be with you for most of your life. Women learn early to push the hormone driven whiplash of romantic longing and PMS into the background and live their live as civilized humans. Anyone who deserves to call himself a man learns to master his hormones and his longing as well. Women are wonderfully different, but they are your equals as humans deserving of respect in every way. They are not your sex toys. They do not owe you sex, or respect that you do not earn by being a human who has demonstrated emotional intelligence and respect for them as women and humans. I don't care if you can make it rain like a gangsta or any other kind of player, that will get you little from any but a very limited range of women, and nothing from anyone you want to spend any time with.

Still, boys in our current culture get very distorted images of sex and the expectations of sex, primarily from online porn. And yes, if he hasn't already, you son will almost certainly see plenty of it by the time he reaches high school and beyond. You need to process that reality in your parental mind and control it if you can, both with software on your computer and the sexual discussions you have with your sons.

Somehow we have to convey to our sons that the porn they see online has almost nothing to do with what a girl wants in a relationship or in sex. Now, female sexual desires are as varied as anything else about humans, as we have noted before, and this isn't to say that just like the various tastes people have in food, music, clothes, and movies women don't enthusiastically do those things you see in porn for their own needs, for variety, or to please someone they love. But the vast majority of women find much of the sex in porn to be degrading, difficult, and often painful stunts that no one in their right mind would do on any regular basis. It's not that they don't like sex, even exotic, kinky sex, but like any other self-respecting, intelligent person, they have no desire to be hurt, abused, and degraded. Unfortunately, for many boys nowadays, exactly that type of porn sex is what they think is normal and what they demand from girls. Boys have to get over that outlook, and that starts with the example and conversations we set as parents.

As noted previously, all that advice about women needing attention, humor, and conversation really is true. Relationship building, trust, and respect is as much a part of female nature as is the urge to conquer and dominate in boys and young men. Those warm fuzzy things nurture their sexuality and build attraction. Sadomasochistic sexual demands from the get-go simply won't do it. Historically, it often takes men well into their adulthood (if then) to clearly understand this, and we resist it even then. When a boy grows up absorbing the increasingly sadomasochistic brand of porn that they see online, along with the sense of instant sexual gratification that porn and our media culture imply, it stacks the deck even further against two young people getting each other as people, and not as sex toy and master. Yet this difference between entertainment/fantasy perception and the real life nature of women is exactly what we have to convey and re-teach to our young men.

And of course, despite our bravado, young men both need and make powerful emotional connections from sex too. Undeniably we men are built in such a way that we *can* enjoy sex recreationally and without connection. That does *not* mean that we are immune to serious emotional attachment in sexual relationships as well as the nurturing and connection traditionally associated with women. Sex and orgasm triggers the release of powerful endorphin chemicals in the brain that bind two people together emotionally. Girls/women need and seek more of this emotional connection in relationships first, usually before sexual connection, but boys and men can be devastated by it. Compared to young men, girls rarely do dangerously impulsive, suicidal, or murderous acts in connection with breakups (though I did have a girlfriend who secretly destroyed all the zippers in my pants when I broke it off—poetic, no doubt, but it made for a very traumatic post breakup business trip as I realized I had with me no functioning pants to wear..) while almost daily one sees in the news some murder or suicide, or both, committed by a distraught young man in romantic agony. Girls can be emotionally traumatic to be around; boys can be emotionally dangerous and scary. Again, almost all of this is made worse when sex starts at younger ages, and is exacerbated when boys think that the sadomasochistic sex they see online is the norm.

So, we need to teach our young men to reacquire at least a bit of the "putting women on a pedestal" thing that started fading away in the sexual revolution of the 60s. The idea of respecting women and their uniqueness needs to be re-introduced and emphasized. Just as a young man demands respect for his male accomplishments and prowess at whatever he pursues, girls and their social skill sets and the counterbalance they provide to male nature (let alone their ability to reproduce) must be held as a treasure, not just a vessel for male desire. I know, fat chance, but we have to point consistently in that direction if we are to try and help them earn maturity and sexual wisdom. We can strive to teach a healthy trade off of respect and honor for the "fair sex" while allowing women the freedom and opportunities they deserve and have earned the last 50 years.

But how? The first generation of young men who grew up on porn are now moving into fatherhood, while those slightly older have middle school children (and certainly a history with porn that their fathers never had). What do we say and do to raise young men and women with a healthy, intelligent take on life and sex? Do we know ourselves well enough to do that?

The young fathers with baby daughters growing into their teens will make this connection very rapidly. As comedian Chris Rock says about holding his baby daughter for the first time, "I mean, they don't grade fathers. But if your daughter's a stripper, you f---d up." There is a reason fathers are protective of their daughters. Fathers are guys; they know what young guys are thinking when they see boys looking at their blossoming middle school daughters, so it's no surprise fathers (and very often, big brothers) tend to be very proactive in seeing that their daughters are protected. Still, it is almost invariably the mom who has "the talk" with the daughter, and it's mom who really needs to be able discuss all the issues raised here: the plumbing, boys, sex, the consequences and responsibilities of sex including pregnancy, STDs and then, yes, alternatives to sex such as masturbation. Fathers should be in the discussion too, but it doesn't seem to work out that way very often. Certainly, if you are the single father of a daughter, you too have to suck it up and confront this part of your daughter's life. If you want to know how to approach this, I refer you again to Dr. Laura Berman (footnote/appendix).

As to sons, I can't claim great experience other than my own as a boy since my wife and I raised daughters. But, having raised daughters and having been a boy grown to some level of mature adulthood (most of the time) I know what I would want a son to know about how to treat girls and women.

To begin, I would tell my sons that, as Aretha said, they simply must show girls "a little respect." However much we hear about the demise of western civilization and the male's place in it, it is still very much a man's world. Guys will still on average make more money and have more freedom in their life choices than women for the foreseeable future. "Women and children first" remains the central tenet of any successful culture (Heinlein again), and the protection of women and the proper raising of offspring remain the real purpose of our species and its institutions. The male drive for success in career, finance, sports, and war all come back to the competition for resources to attract mates and raise families. In short, guys, you do it all for the girls in the end, and anybody who wants to be a rock god or sports star knows instinctively that the girls (or readily available sex of any kind, straight or gay) are part of the deal. It's just that the taking care of them and raising their children part has become a little lost lately. While undeniably there is a certain proportion of the female population that will aggressively pursue successful men sexually, feeding the fantasies of all young men, it simply doesn't work that way for most men or women. Never has, never will. Women expect to be courted, pursued, and made to feel desired and worthwhile, and if they expect to be successful with women, young men and boys must make that fact a reality of their life. It's both that simple and the most difficult aspect of human relations for boys and men to really get.

I would tell my sons that girl's social need for connection dominates their interaction. Anyone who has been around 14 year old girls soon realizes that talking is so wrapped up in their social interaction that it's like breathing. It is instinctive and even unconscious, so deep is this need to communicate and build social bridges. All teachers have had the experience of halting a lecture or class discussion to get the attention of two or more girls chattering in whispers in some part of the room. And all teachers have seen the wounded, genuinely innocent expression on the girls' faces as they say in unison "but we weren't talking..." and realize that they truly are not aware of what they are doing on an intellectual, cognizant level; they were just connecting. As I often say, "yes you *were* talking. It's part of your breathing process." Boys will rarely deny talking, because they were doing it for a specific purpose, not as part of an unconscious social networking instinct.

Paying attention to this social need in girls can not only help boys connect with girls, but can reap social rewards as well. Girls and women are much more socially observant and generally have a much better feeling for social situations. All that chatter is a social radar that can help any boy and man navigate social and eventually corporate cultures successfully. To twist Steve Harvey's advice, "Think Like a Lady, Act Like a Man" can work both ways. (38) Like most things in human relations, the more you understand some aspect of it (in this case, women and girls), the more you appreciate it and the less likely you are to hurt and be hurt.

So there you have it. You are wonderful, thoughtful, heroic teens, or you are the parents of one—which is certainly more than heroic. Sex and sexuality is a big part of life. Prepare for it like any other part of life, whether it is a career, sports, driving, or college. Like most important and desirable things in life, it is very much double-edged, giving us the greatest pleasure along with life-long and life threatening consequences. There is no such thing as too much knowledge if it is presented honestly, responsibly, and completely, the good with the bad. In sexuality, only the withholding of knowledge, for whatever well-meaning reason, can lead to harm. Kids: respect yourself and respect your parents. When they seem to be insane, that's the very time their love and concern for you is right there in your face, because they were like you once, and they want to protect you from the passions you are experiencing. Parents: love your children (not that there is any doubt) enough to remember what it's like to be them. Then fight like hell to protect them, while letting them stretch and grow.

Now parents, go out there and teach them all you've read above (or give them this book) and/or demand that your school district do it properly so that all students are protected by real knowledge, not just cultural wishful thinking....

The very best of good fortune and wisdom to all of you......

WOMAN

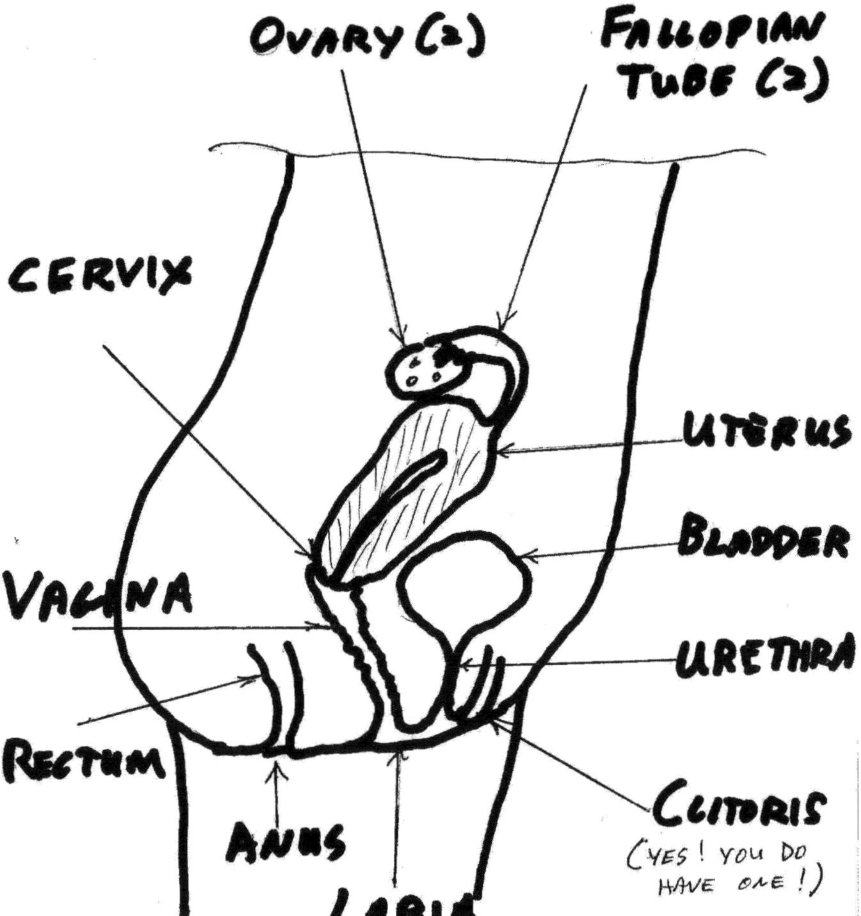
OVARY (2)
FALLOPIAN TUBE (2)
CERVIX
UTERUS
BLADDER
VAGINA
URETHRA
RECTUM
CLITORIS
(YES! YOU DO HAVE ONE!)
ANUS
LABIA

MAN

VAS
DEFERENS

BLADDER

SEMINAL
VESICLE

PROSTATE
GLAND

COWPERS
GLAND

URETHRA

PENIS

RECTUM

ANUS

TESTIS
OR
TESTICLE

PENISES!

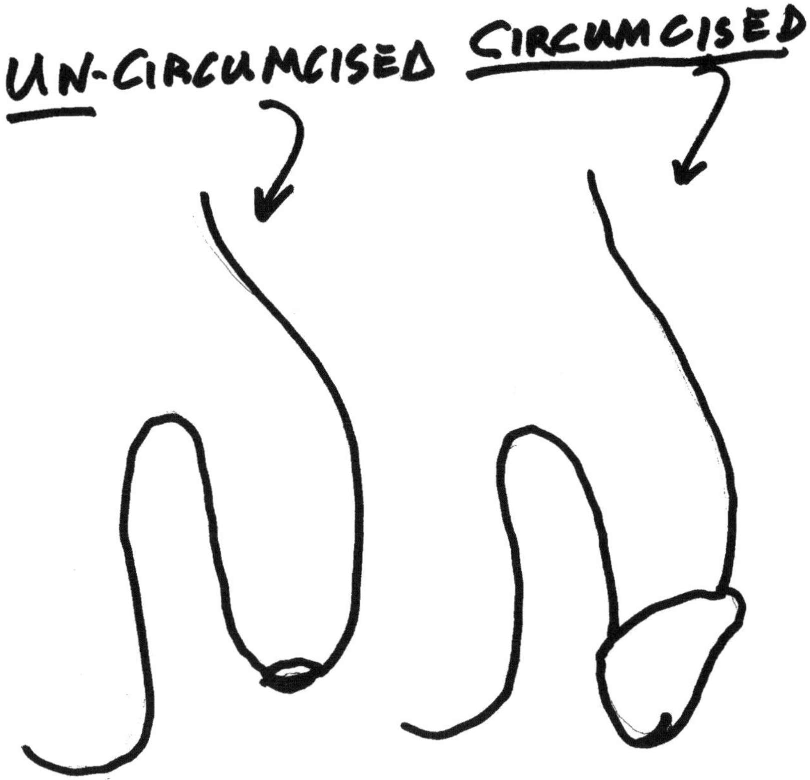

BIBLIOGRAPHY

1. "Managing Kids Search Queries: What Parents Need to Know." *Common Sense Media,* January 8, 2010, http://www.commonsensemedia.org/new/managing-kids-search-queries-what-parents-need-know
    Note: Read the entire article and the links showing the entire top 100 search list. Check out the directors and advisors to this credible site as well as a lot of other good media savvy information for parents and educators.

2. "Middle School Youth as Young as 12 Engaging in Risky Sexual Activity." *Science Daily,* April 10, 2009, http://www.sciencedaily.com/releases/2009/04/090408145354.htm.

3. Abstinence and Abstinence Only Education: A review of U.S. policies and programs; *Journal of Adolescent Health,* 38 (2006) 72-8; available at: http://www.moappp.org/Documents/articles/2006/SantelliAbstinenceonlyEducationReviewPaper.pdf

4. Castleman, Michael. "Penis Size: How To Make the Most of What You've Got, and How Best to Please Women With It." Available at: http://www.mcastleman.com/page3/page41/page57/page60/page60.html2.

5.   Anitai, Stefan. "This Man Has the Largest Penis In The World: 13.5 in (32.29 cm) Erect!" *Softpedia*, http://news.softpedia.com/news/This-Man-Has-the-Largest-Penis-in-the-World-13-5-in-34-29-cm-erect-76722.shtml.

6.   Hunt, Stephan. "Do 'Penis Size' Studies Measure Up?" Available at EXN.CA. http://www.psurg.com/discovery2001.html.

7.   Santucci, Richard A. MD, FACS. "Penile Fracture and Trauma." e-Medicine from WebMD. Available at: http://emedicine.medscape.com/article/456305-overview. (**Warning**: Graphic images of messed up penises sure to thrill, gross-out, horrify, and delight teenagers.)

8.   Gordon, Serena. "Circumcision Guards Against STDs." *US News and World Report, "Health Day"* March 25, 2009. Available at: http://health.usnews.com/health-news/family-¹health/womens-health/articles/2009/03/25/circumcision-guards-against-stds.

9.   American Psychological Association. "Sexualization of Girls." Available at http://www.apa.org/pi/women/programs/girls/report.aspx.

10.   Marlowe, Frank. "The Nubility Hypothesis The Human Breast as an Honest Signal of Residual Reproductive Value." Available at: http://www.anthro.fsu.edu/people/faculty/marlowe_pubs/nubility.pdf.

11.   Caro, T.M. "Human Breasts: Unsupported Hypotheses Reviewed." *Springer Link*. Available at: http://www.springerlink.com/content/gk34152k55505x20/.

12.   Rey, Rudolfo & Josso, Nathalie. "Chapter 7. Sexual Differentiation." Available from Endotext.com at http://

www.endotext.org/pediatrics/pediatrics7/pediatrics-frame7.htm.

13. Long, John A. "Dawn of the Deed." *Scientific American*, January 2011, issue 35.

14. Berman, Dr. Laura. "Dr. Berman's Sex Talk (and associated links and videos)." The *Oprah Winfrey Show* website. Available at: http://myown.oprah.com/search/index. html?q=Dr.%20Berman%27s%20sex%20talk.

15. Wikipedia. "Pubic Hair." Wikipedia doesn't always have a great reputation as a source. What *is* valuable, however, is the list of sources and links used in the Wikipedia articles. These are often extensive and should be checked out. Available at: http://en.wikipedia.org/wiki/Pubic_hair

16. Dawn Stacey, M.Ed, LMHC. "Double-bagging Condoms." Available at: http://contraception.about. com/b/2011/01/13/double-bagging-condoms.htm.

17. ABC News Health. "Study Reports Anal Sex On Rise Among Teens." Available at: http://abcnews.go.com/ Health/story?id=6428003&page=1.

18. National Campaign to Prevent Teen Pregnancy. "Teen Pregnancy, Poverty and Income Disparity." Available at: http://www.thenationalcampaign.org/why-it-matters/ pdf/poverty.pdf.

19. March of Dimes. "Teenage Pregnancy." Available at: http://www.marchofdimes.com/professionals/medical-resources_teenpregnancy.html.

20. Center for Disease Control. "Male Latex Condoms and Sexually Transmitted Disease." Available at: http://www.cdc.gov/condomeffectiveness/latex.htm.

21. "Healthy Strokes." Available at: http://www.healthystrokes.com/youngfem.html.

22. "Dr. Laura Berman on Female Ejaculation Video." Available at: http://www.oprah.com/relationships/Dr-Laura-Berman-on-Female-Ejaculation-Video.

23. Kerner, Ian. "Understanding female's sexual fluidity" CNN Health, available at: http://thechart.blogs.cnn.com/2012/02/09/understanding-females-sexual-fluidity/

24. Diamond, Lisa M. **Sexual Fluidity**, Harvard University Press, 2009

25. Wikipedia. "Female Ejaculation." Available at: http://en.wikipedia.org/wiki/Female_ejaculation. *Note particularly the extensive list of references and links in the bibliography of this Wikipedia entry for more information.*

26. Mayo Clinic. "Toxic Shock Syndrome." Available at: http://www.mayoclinic.com/health/toxic-shock-syndrome/DS0022.

27. "What the Gay Brain Looks Like." *TIME/CNN Health and Science*, Tuesday, June 17, 2008. http://www.time.com/time/health/article/0,8599,1815538,00.html.

28. "Brain Study Shows Differences Between Gays, Straights" *The Washington Post,* June 23, 2008, page A-12. A different report on the same study above from TIME/CNN

29.   Brain Research Institute UCLA. "What Makes People Gay" Available at: http://www.bri.ucla.edu/bri_weekly/news_050812.asp

30.   Heinlen, Robert & Vassallo, D.F. <u>The Notebooks of Lazarus Long,</u> Toronto: Longman Canada Limited, 1973.
        Note: The late Robert Heinlein has long been considered one of true giants of science fiction, and some of his work stepped out of the genre to become literary as well as cult classics. Many baby boomers read *Stranger in a Strange Land* in college. Topping that work in richness and variety of theme, character, and setting, *Time Enough For Love*, published in 1973, is the source of the quotes used in this work. The novel is the memoirs of the 2000 year old Lazarus Long, ancestor of most of living humanity 2000 years in the future. Running through the work are sections called the "Notebooks of Lazarus Long" with his truly priceless observations on human nature, life, and love. These are so beloved that they have been broken out into separate, stand-alone booklets. One of many editions is listed in the footnote above. New and used editions can be readily found on Amazon.com.

31.   "Sex Infections Found in Quarter of Teenage Girls." *The New York Times*, March 12, 2008. Available at: http://www.nytimes.com/2008/03/12/science/12std.html.

32.   The Oprah website. "Having the Sex Talk With Your Kids," and "Dr. Laura Berman on Masturbation Video" where Berman talks to a mother whose 4 year old daughter is starting to explore her body. http://www.oprah.com/relationships/Download-Dr-Laura-Bermans-Talking-to-Kids-About-Sex-Handbook

33.   Fairness and Accuracy In Reporting (FAIR). "Bashing Youth." U.S. Public Health Service statistics on teen pregnancies, March-April 1994. Available at: http://www.fair.org/index.php?page=1224.

34.   "The Big Question: Why Are Teenage Birthrates So High, and What Can Be Done About It?" *The Independent,* 17 February, 2009. Available at: http://www.independent.co.uk/extras/big-question/the-big-question-why-are-teenage-pregnancy-rates-so-high-and-what-can-be-done-about-it-1623828.html.

35.   Advocates for Youth. "The Case for a Rights, Respect, Responsibility Approach." This site is dedicated to a sex ed approach for teens and parents similar to that espoused in this book, so naturally the author is a fan. Read this article, judge the graphs and statistics for yourself, and note particularly the extensive references and links at the end of the article. Available at: http://www.advocatesforyouth.org/publications/publications-a-z/419-adolescent-sexual-health-in-europe-and-the-us.

36.   Eric Spitsnagel, "How Internet Porn is Changing Teen Sex," *Details*, March 2013, available at: http://www.details.com/sex-relationships/porn-and-perversions/200907/how-internet-porn-is-changing-teen-sex

37.   Michael Castleman, "How Does Internet Porn Affect Teens -- Really?", *Psychology Today,* May 17, 2011, Available at: http://www.psychologytoday.com/blog/all-about-sex/201105/how-does-internet-porn-affect-teens-really

38.   Steve Harvey, *Act Like a Lady, Think Like a Man,* 2009, Harper Collins, ISBN 97-0-06-172898-3

Made in the USA
San Bernardino, CA
16 September 2014